NOT MY KIND OF MENNONITE

BY

MARIA MOORE

Maria Moore
Truth will always = peace

 FriesenPress

One Printers Way
Altona, MB R0G 0B0
Canada

www.friesenpress.com

Copyright © 2023 by Maria Moore
First Edition — 2023

All rights reserved.

No part of this publication may be reproduced in any form, or by any means, electronic or mechanical, including photocopying, recording, or any information browsing, storage, or retrieval system, without permission in writing from FriesenPress.

ISBN
978-1-03-917545-7 (Hardcover)
978-1-03-917544-0 (Paperback)
978-1-03-917546-4 (eBook)

1. BIOGRAPHY & AUTOBIOGRAPHY, RELIGIOUS

Distributed to the trade by The Ingram Book Company

This book is based on a true story.

CONTENT WARNING: There is material in this book that can be difficult. This includes: murder, rape and sexual assault, child abuse, mental health and addictions. Please look after yourself and seek help if you need it. Canada Suicide Prevention Service 1-833-456-4566

Dedicated to my father, George (Gerhard) Peters

The Gentle Giant

1939–1972

In memory of George Peters.

ANNA'S FAMILY

PARENTS

Johan (Jacob)   Maria

CHILDREN

Jacob	Heinrich	Sarah
Johann	Katherina	Anna
Maria	Helena	Agatha
Heinrich	Heinrich	
Heinrich	Gerhard	

GEORGE'S FAMILY

PARENTS

Jacob   Gertruda

CHILDREN

Wilhelm   Peter   George

Johan   Jacob

GEORGE AND ANNA'S FAMILY

PARENTS

George   Anna

CHILDREN

Gertruda	Maria	John
Jacob (Jake)	Maria	Isaak
George Jr.	Peter	

PROLOGUE

Not *My Kind of Mennonite* took several years to complete, with intervals of newspaper archival research, meetings with persons of interest, and connecting with relatives that remembered me but who I had no recollection of. There would be many awkward conversations with people, but after meeting me and hearing my memories of my life, people would share what they had heard or experienced with my father and his murder. My first languages were Plautdietsch and German, but with so many years living in an English family and school system, I no longer had the tools to communicate with many of my Old Colony Mennonite family members. This research revealed a need for me to better understand the Old Colony Mennonites, specifically the Manitoba Colony's history and progress from Prussia to Manitoba and then to northern Mexico.

My book is based on the true story of my parents' lives and encounters. The stories within come from a combination of friends and relatives who all provided a small glimpse for me of what their lives looked like on a day-to-day basis. I can only write my stories and experiences as they were told to me and recalled by various relatives. My story is not the story of my siblings. Each of us had our own journey through abuse, trauma, and foster care, and my intent is not to take their story or voice from them by assuming we had the same experiences.

Growing up, I was able to meet various biological family members and learn the stories that were shared between my cousins, aunts, and uncles to justify why we were all taken away and put up for adoption and into foster care. These stories were shared between families in all languages and eventually changed to

PROLOGUE

fit the needs of each generation. I have learned from textbooks and memories about my heritage as a Mennonite and my strict early years of religious education. I developed a deeper understanding of generational trauma and post-traumatic stress disorder (PTSD) in my own exploration of my past through education and personal research. The abuse and trauma of my childhood would surface unexpectedly with various triggers through my life and lead me to journal, explore, and find ways to process the information and find a way to let it live in the past and teach me about the future. It was not my fault.

I have researched Mennonites since the age of nine, when I was adopted. In farmers' markets and local Mennonite communities, I would look into faces, trying to find a resemblance or connection with them. I have come to discover that instead of not being their kind of Mennonite from their specific region or church, I am a mixture of all. I come from several hundred years of Anabaptist followers, but also pioneers, mathematicians, teachers, engineers, land surveyors, farmers, mothers, bakers, writers, and nurses. We are all one nation of Mennonites finding our way, and I am getting closer all the time.

CHAPTER ONE:
THE SHOOTING

January 1972

George, with his hands in the sink, turned to look around the Vienna Hotel bar. He was a tall man, standing just over six feet, five inches tall, and had to lean over to wash glasses in the sink. He stood straight and stretched his shoulders back to relieve the tension at the end of his shift. It had been a great one. It was just the three of them left to close that night, he, Frenchy, and Cameron. The owner, Ronny, had decided to head home early. Working at the hotel bar gave George hope that life in Ontario was going to be good this time. The guys all treated him like he was a local, and he could laugh and joke with them when he was at work.

As he finished the last glass and dried the remainder of the dishes, he looked around to see only a few locals left. The usual crowd at the bar was a combination of tobacco farmers and their wives, farm labourers, and store owners. George had started working here after coming to Ontario from Mexico to work in the greenhouses and tobacco barns. This job gave him respect, making him part of the community instead of "one of them." He could make conversation easily with the patrons, and it hadn't been very long before they'd all accepted him. He wasn't a hired hand but a real employee, in charge of drinks, cleaning up, and making sure everyone treated each other properly.

One of the things that George loved about the job was the smells people brought with them. He remembered working in the soil as a small child,

CHAPTER ONE: THE SHOOTING

laughing with his brothers and cousins. The scent of dirt on the farmers and labourers made it feel like the olden days, and it warmed his heart. That night, he could smell a mix of cigarette smoke, tobacco harvest, and dirt as he walked around the bar with his tin garbage can, emptying ashtrays and chatting with those that remained.

"Last call. Need anything else before we close?" he asked with a smile. Everyone declined except one man George had seen in the hotel only a few times.

"Sure, I'll have another," the man said.

George looked him over. He was a pretty good judge of character and could tell if someone needed to be cut off for the night. This guy wasn't a local but wore work clothes, so he must have been working at the farms. It wasn't unusual to have new people in every day, with all the local farmers needing migrant workers to get their crops harvested and ready to sell.

George nodded to him and finished with his ashtrays and wiping the tables. As the others left, the man walked to the bar to have a seat while he waited for George to pour him another beer. After serving him the drink, George headed to the corner of the bar to call Gerhard and Margaret, his brother- and sister-in-law, on the pay phone.

"Hello. I'm coming around when I'm done work to get the kids. We can have a drink to ring in the New Year. No need to get all angry with me. They're my kids, and it's time they come home. What? No, wait. It'll be late when I get there because I need to close up tonight, but I'm definitely coming. Get the kids ready." George shook his head to himself. His sister-in-law wasn't being very cooperative. Anna, his wife, had taken the kids to live with her brother and his family over a month ago after George had gotten angry with her. George had recently found out that his wife was again performing sexual acts around town with various men instead of caring for the kids. He'd been working hard at the bar, and with tips and extra shifts, he had saved up enough to get a decent house to rent and bring his children with him. The kids would be safer there. Hanging up the phone, he grabbed the tea towel and started drying dishes as he thought over the next steps and how much better life was going to be afterward.

Frenchy and Cameron finished restocking the fridge and got ready to head out. "You okay to finish up, George?" one of them asked.

George checked on the lone man at the bar and nodded in their direction. "I'm okay here. Thanks for your help tonight." They looked in the direction of the man and raised their eyebrows. He nodded again to let them know it was all under control. When the others left, George turned to the man. "I'm George."

"I'm Marshy," the stranger answered. "You got some troubles? Couldn't help but overhear you on the phone."

"I hope not. I'm heading over to have a drink with my in-laws after work, and then I'm going to pick my kids up. My wife took them over there, and it's time they came home."

"Going to have any trouble with getting them?" asked Marshy.

"No. I called to let him know that I'll get them tonight. They've been there long enough. If their *mutti* wants to stay, she can, but the kids need to come home."

At Gerhard's home, his wife, Margaret, had just hung up the phone. She could feel her heart racing and face flushing as she caught her breath. "Gerhard," she yelled.

Gerhard had been reading the newspaper in the front room and got up to his wife's voice. "What's going on?" he asked flatly.

Margaret quickly explained that George was coming for the kids. "I told him not to, but he's coming. I'm sure he's probably drunk, especially coming from that hotel."

"If that's the case, there's no way he's getting in this house. I'll call the police."

His sister, Anna, had come to his house with her six children over a month ago. She wasn't getting along with her husband, and Gerhard felt stuck in the middle. Anna had told him that George was violent and would hurt her and the children often, so he felt protective. He wanted to defend his sister, but George was his friend, and he'd never seen the man raise a hand to any of them. It was also getting difficult to support everyone, with six children and a wife of his own.

Concerned about the situation, Gerhard walked quickly to the telephone. He could hear the chatter of kids upstairs, even though it was late. All of the kids' beds were on the floor, and it took a while for them to settle down and fall asleep. He dialed the police.

5

CHAPTER ONE: THE SHOOTING

"OPP. Do you have an emergency?" asked the operator.

"I'm Gerhard Wolf, and my brother-in-law, George, is headed over here. He's drunk and belligerent and is not getting in this house. His kids are here, but he's not fit to have them. If you guys don't stop him, I'll shoot him."

Anna had told Gerhard about George forcing her to have sex with men around town for money and booze for his addiction. Gerhard was protective of his sister and her family, and so Anna's stories about her marriage and life were troubling. Gerhard didn't want his wife to be upset, and he knew that he would have to confront George, which made him anxious. He and George had built a strong bond over the years, but things had changed when they came to Canada. They had drifted apart in their beliefs and values.

The dispatcher asked for his address. He already knew the name, as Gerhard had called the week before with the same problem when George wanted to see his children. "How do you know he's coming?" asked the dispatcher.

"He called my wife from the bar and said he was coming over. She said he was drunk and is bringing more alcohol to our house. We won't have it. A good man would know not to be tempted by alcohol and all the sins that it can make you do. He can't come in, and I'll shoot him if I have to," Gerhard repeated.

"Now, don't shoot him. I'll send an officer over right away. If you shoot him, you could get in serious trouble." The dispatcher hung up.

George looked at the clock in the bar. 1:30. He finished cleaning up and chatting with Marshy.

"You want to have a drink since you're almost done your shift?" Marshy asked.

"No, I can't. One of the main rules here is that there's no drinking on the job." George knew that in order for him to keep his position, he had to follow the rules of the hotel. The owners had been really good to him and trusted him, so he wasn't going to risk his job or their business. Through them, he was going to have a better life for his kids.

"You need some company to go and get your kids?"

George looked at Marshy and remembered that his own car was having trouble starting in the cold weather. "Sure. We can pick up the kids and then take them home. It's only a few miles' drive."

Ron was the OPP officer who got the call from dispatch about Gerhard Wolf. He remembered similar calls when George had gone over to see his kids. It was hard sometimes to get the full story, as Gerhard would be angry and revert to his first language, Plautdietsch, when he got flustered.

Ron called Gerhard to get a better idea of how real the threat was of George coming to the house and Gerhard wanting to shoot him. Gerhard was upset and angry, and it took a while to get him settled down enough to get the whole story. Ron assured him that he would do everything he could to find George and warn him that he would be charged with trespassing if he went to the residence that night.

"If you don't find him, I'll kill him," repeated Gerhard. Ron told him there would be severe consequences if he shot someone, and Gerhard had simply replied, "I don't care!" Ron hung up the phone and went out to his police car to start his search for George. Gerhard told him what his car looked like and where he lived and worked. The snow was still blowing, making visibility very hard on the country roads. Ron checked out the old schoolhouse where George lived with his family to see if he had come to his senses and gone home, but no lights were on.

"How many kids you got?" Marshy asked.

"Six of them," George said with a smile. He loved being a *vati* (father), and he wanted the best for his kids in Canada. As he reflected over the past year with Anna's mental health breakdowns and her behaviour of disappearing with strangers, he felt the trip tonight to get his children was urgent. George could feel tension building in his neck and shoulders just thinking about it. Marshy finished the last swig of his beer while George was careful to clean, count the money, and lock up the Vienna Hotel. He stepped out into the cold, proud that the owners, Ronny and Dorothy, trusted him and that he knew things would be okay for the starting shift tomorrow at noon.

George curled himself up to get into the passenger seat of Marshy's car and shivered. It was a cold night, and snow was blowing. Back in the Chihuahua Hills, it could get cold in the winter months, but this Canadian cold was

CHAPTER ONE: THE SHOOTING

different, and he still wasn't used to it. The front seat was littered with beer bottles, and there was a six-pack partially frozen beneath his feet. As the car started, Marshy turned on the heat and shouted over the fan to "grab me a beer and have one yourself." George nodded, handed an open beer to Marshy, opened one himself, and took a big drink. The ice in the bottle was refreshing.

The flakes were coming down in big, wet drops when Marshy turned the car around and spun his tires to get out of the parking lot. "Which way?" he asked. "I don't know my way around here." George pointed to the left, and the car spun as it turned down Nova Scotia Line, west of Port Burwell. He could hardly see the road with all the drifting. The big ditches on each side of the road were now part of the white landscape. Marshy had his hands tight on the steering wheel as he asked George what his wife was doing, taking the kids away from home.

Ron had gone back to the station, as he could find no sign of George. He'd gone to the Vienna Hotel, but the lights were out, and George's empty car was in the parking lot. The weather was terrible, and he figured the family domestic call might work out to be nothing.

Looking at the map in the station, he found Gerhard's house on a concession road, past where his detachment would normally cover. Ron called his sergeant. Based on the jurisdiction markings on the map at Tillsonburg, the sergeant told Ron that he was absolutely right. He should stay in the Burwell office and monitor the phone until the sergeant could reach the St. Thomas OPP detachment. Once they had an officer in the area, St. Thomas would contact Ron and let him know.

St. Thomas called back fairly quickly and got directions from Ron to the Wolf residence, along with Gerhard's telephone number so they could let him know the OPP number that he should be using. Once the St. Thomas officer arrived in the vicinity of the Wolf residence, they could stay in contact with Ron over their police car radios. The St. Thomas officer went to the Wolf residence and talked with Gerhard, collected information about what was going on, and informed Gerhard that he would talk to the Port Burwell officer and see if, between the two of them searching, they couldn't track George down.

George was anxious in the passenger seat, holding onto the door handle. The roads were slippery, and the car's back end kept swaying. He knew that getting his kids from Gerhard's was going to be hard. They had been angry with him when he was last there at Christmas. Anna had been filling their heads full of stories, and he was getting tired of defending himself. He knew that what Anna was saying about him wasn't right, but he also knew that her brother would believe her, as his pride would make it impossible to think that she might have been telling him lies. He kept an eye on the snow, knowing they would have to turn soon to get to the nursery's farmhouse. Gerhard was living there and working at the greenhouse, and Anna had walked there a few weeks ago with the kids. He had to make a move that night to save his children. Even though the car would be crowded, he could fit all six of them in and get them back home safely.

Gerhard went upstairs after the OPP left and found his .22 caliber rifle. He brought it down and Margaret saw him. "I'll scare him off with this. We need this to stop, and the police won't help us, so we have to protect ourselves." Gerhard loaded the rifle and put it in the closet beside the front door.

Marshy turned when he was told, and they pulled in front of the house. George wanted to take care of things on his own, but maybe, if he had Marshy with him, it might soften the mood and make things a bit easier. "Don't stay out here in the cold. Bring a few beers. We'll go in and visit before we get the kids."

Marshy grabbed the alcohol and followed him to the door. George knocked loudly and then heard his sister-in-law Margaret yell through the wood. "You go home. You won't be coming in here tonight. The police are looking for you."

"I'm here to celebrate the New Year with you and Gerhard." He could hear muffled sounds behind the door. Standing with his coat pulled around his ears to keep warm, he looked down at Marshy, who was grinning with the beer tucked in his jacket. The door unlocked, and Margaret and Gerhard stood before them. George walked in with Marshy on his heels.

"Hey. How are you? Happy new year," George offered.

Gerhard said nothing. He looked around George and saw Marshy. "You're not welcome here, and you can't come in. You have to go home."

CHAPTER ONE: THE SHOOTING

Marshy spoke up. "We're only here to have a New Year's drink with you." Gerhard moved to block George from coming in, slightly pushing him in the direction of the door. George resisted, and Gerhard was thrown off-balance, making him stagger into Margaret, who fell against the wall. This startled Gerhard, who turned to see his wife struggling. George stepped around them and into the house, yelling up the stairs. "George, Jake, Gertruda, Maria. Let's go home and get Peter and Johnny." He could tell a nice visit wasn't going to happen, but at least he could bring his children home.

As George walked to the central staircase and looked up, he could see shadows of the bare bulb against the wall. A door opened at the top of the stairs, and he could hear the sound of children as he took a few steps up in anticipation of his kids coming down. Behind him, Gerhard had regained his balance, reached into the corner, and took out his loaded gun. Marshy watched from the threshold as George moved up the stairs and Gerhard raised the gun. He was still taking in the scene when Gerhard fired the bullet.

All the kids were sleeping upstairs on the floor, but Maria could hear her vati calling. She watched as the cousins hid under their blankets in various corners of the room, but her siblings all stood to leave. Her mutti, Anna, was hiding in the closet behind the clothing, avoiding a potential confrontation and the risk that her lies would be revealed. Maria kept moving toward the doorway, her brothers in line behind her, even though her cousin Agatha tried to pull her back.

George was walking up the stairs, saw Maria's eyes, and called for her with a strained smile on his face. Maria stepped into the hallway just as her uncle raised the gun in the air. The noise alerted George, who turned around to face him. It was the first time she had seen a gun in real life. Focusing on her vati's voice once more, she started down the stairs toward him. A loud explosion startled her, and she covered her ears, only to see her vati lying on the stairs. "Get back in that room," shouted her uncle. She was shocked and scared and wanted to go to her vati.

George had turned to meet Gerhard's eyes just as he had fired the bullet. He felt the sharp pain as the bullet entered his left shoulder, and he turned once again toward his children up the stairs. He was in pain, and blood was on the stairs. Maria's older cousin grabbed her arm and pulled her back into the bedroom. By now, all the children were awake, and many were crying. Anna remained quiet in the closet.

Crying, yelling, and moaning filled the house, even as Maria and the other children went to the bedroom window to look outside into the darkness. She could see headlights to a car and watched as her uncle kicked her vati down the front door steps and he fell into the snow. He staggered to the car, leaving a trail of blood as he struggled to get inside. She watched the stuck car move back and forth to free itself and then speed down the road. Where was her vati? She felt abandoned, fearful, and confused. The house was alive now with yelling and tears.

Finally, Anna opened the closet door and crawled out. "What's going on? What was that noise?" Her children and nieces and nephews were all looking out the window, and she walked over to see that was going on. She could see the blood on the snow and the car pulling out. She didn't understand and turned to walk downstairs and see her brother and sister-in-law. Her screams sounded through the house as she saw the blood on the stairs and smelled the gun smoke still lingering.

Gerhard reached for the telephone on the wall and dialed the police. The St. Thomas officer got a radio message from his detachment dispatch, stating that they had just received a call from a Gerhard Wolf saying that they'd be able to find his brother-in-law now because he'd just shot him. George had taken off in the car, but Gerhard still had the gun.

When the gun fired and the yelling started, Marshy had run out to the car and started it. He was trying to decide if he would just take off or wait for George. Alcohol and the cold clouded his mind. He could see George coming out of the house, though, and then Gerhard pushed him into the snow. Blood stained the white in the light of the single outside bulb as George picked himself up and shuffled to the car. Marshy leaned over and opened the door to let him in.

"Holy shit, George. What the hell happened?" asked Marshy as he struggled to get the car moving. He looked at George, who was holding his stomach. George was a big, strong man, but all of a sudden, he looked weak and frail. Marshy could feel his heart racing and panic setting in. He didn't like the sight of blood.

CHAPTER ONE: THE SHOOTING

George sat quietly, trying to piece together what to do next. He could feel the sharp pain in his neck and chest, and it increased with each breath. He leaned against the door and took a few more big breaths as he listened to Marshy panic and try to make sense of the next steps. "I need to go to the hospital," he finally said. "I've been shot."

Marshy put his foot on the gas and accelerated. As he gripped the steering wheel and tried to move forward, he was afraid that whoever had the gun in the house would be coming out to finish the job and then kill him too. He was desperate to get out of there. On the road, the visibility was next to nil. The snow blew right into the windshield, and Marshy could hardly see the hood of the car. He looked back and forth to see if he recognized anything familiar but didn't wait. He just wanted to be out of there.

Ron received a call from St. Thomas OPP, asking him to stay out on the roads and see if he could find George's vehicle because they believed George had been shot.

Marshy didn't know where to go. He thought of his friend's place in Port Burwell and decided to head there. He would know what to do. He just needed to remember where to turn and what road it was on. Goddamn, it was snowy, and he could hear George's breathing, panting, and moaning. If only he hadn't drank so much, he would have been able to think it through. The darkness of the country side roads allowed only the headlights to illuminate his path, and because it was after midnight, no farms had lights on. He could see only blackness when he tried to figure out which way to turn, increasing his panic. His heart was racing, and his mouth was dry. He turned left and went down a side road, finding a big snowdrift. He swerved to miss it and lost control of the car on the underlayer of ice, slamming it sideways into a bunch of pine trees on the driver's side. The car was wedged tightly against the trees and wouldn't move.

Marshy pounded on the steering wheel. "Damn. Damn." He shifted the car from drive to reverse over and over and couldn't move even an inch. Finally, he opened the door, and the wind whistled in, blowing snow across his face.

A light dusting of snow covered George, who was leaning against the car door with his eyes closed.

Marshy couldn't open his door wide enough to get out of the car, so he crawled across George in the passenger seat. Then he helped George get into the back seat to have more space to stretch out. Outside, he kicked the snow from under the tires to try and get more traction. When that was unsuccessful, he came back to his friend. "You stay here, George. I'm going for help, buddy. You're gonna be okay. Any idea where we are, buddy?" Marshy asked anxiously.

George moaned but never opened his eyes. The buzzing in Marshy's head was now on high, and he felt like throwing up. The alcohol from earlier was clouding his thinking even more, and he just felt like running, so he did.

A bird's eye view of the scene would have shown that George was lying only a quarter mile from his house. He was so close to home.

Marshy stepped out of the car into knee-high snow, and the wind caught his open jacket. Zipping it up, he walked; the panic built inside him until he ran. He ran and ran, found a road, and went down it but ended up in a forest. He turned and turned and could see no lights in any direction. If he had stayed on the road, he would have only been five miles from help. Instead, his shortcut through heavily wooded area on an old logging road would eventually come to a dead end. He turned and ran in one direction after another. He felt sick and panicked and could only picture George in the car. The snow was heavy, and he was lost.

It was still dark and snowing when Marshy caught a glimpse of light across a field. He walked toward the light, unable to feel his toes and fingers. It was so cold. He could see that lights were on in the barn and walked through the doors. Despite it being unheated, the warmth of shelter from the wind was welcoming. Frozen and out of breath, Marshy walked between the rooms in the barn until he found a man. "Hey. My friend is shot. He's in the car and needs the hospital. I got stuck. My buddy is in a car, and we got stuck. He needs help, man."

Reg was doing his morning chores that day. He looked at the man in front of him, panicked and nearly frozen. "Slow it down. What is this about someone being shot?" he said slowly.

CHAPTER ONE: THE SHOOTING

Marshy started to tell his story again but could feel panic growing in him. He needed help, and he needed it now. "I need you to drive me to my friend and help him. NOW. He's been shot."

"Slow it down," said Reg. "I'll drive you back the way you came. You tell me what you saw, and I'll get you there. Did you call the police?"

"No. I was in the middle of nowhere. You're the first house I saw."

Reg listened, walking toward the door of the barn. "Let's go to the house and get the truck keys. I don't have a house phone either, but we can take a look and maybe take him to the hospital." Marshy nodded. He wanted to do something, and finally, he could help George.

The cold January wind was blowing snow around the car as George lay inside. Marshy had left the engine running, but it had turned off at some point as George drifted in and out of consciousness. He decided to go for help on his own. He didn't want to die in the car in the ditch. He had a plan to save his family, and he needed to get things moving in the right direction for everyone.

He pushed on the door, opening it and moving the snow to get out. Gusts of wind carried powdery snow, and he could feel the cold and wet air on his face. He still had thick brown hair, and the breeze felt refreshing in the way a swim in Lake Erie would. It wasn't like home in the desert with the mountain streams and the cool evening temperatures. He moved in slow motion to a standing position, even as his mind wandered to his childhood home in Mexico. He coughed and slipped to his side on the ground, the pain taking his breath away. With his feet still in the car, he slowed his breathing down and tried to come up with a plan. Maybe Marshy would be back soon. He could rest until then. He went back in his memories.

His life hadn't been peaceful for a long time. He visualized the red sands of northern Chihuahua, Mexico, as he felt his pulse slow down and peace come over him. This was what he longed for, the simplicity of life when you were just free in the mountains with sun on your face and your brothers and friends around you. He smiled when he thought about being a young boy, riding horses in the desert, chasing snakes, and trapping tarantulas when they came out of their burrows. He could take himself back to that time despite the pain in his chest and the white snow under him turning red from his blood.

Occasionally, George could feel the warmth of his blood running down his chest, quickly followed by cold air and chills. His head was hazy from blood loss and low oxygen levels, but it helped him to slow down the scene and put the pieces together. He pulled his legs out of the car and got himself into a seated position in the snow, leaning his head back to rest for just a little while.

He'd started the day with such good intentions. He'd planned to get his kids, and as he thought of them, he started to cry and take deep breaths, causing the pain to increase. He reached to his ribs to see if he could stop it. His ribs must have broken when the bullet went through. *Damn*, he thought. He tried to focus on other things in his life as he drifted in and out of consciousness. He had flashes of his wedding day, of working with friends in the barns and fields. He loved to watch his children grow and work with him, and he was going to teach them the right way to do things. He had been blessed with many children, but life was a struggle. He sobbed again as he pictured their lives since coming to Canada. It hadn't been easy at the Mennonite colony in Mexico either, but he knew that with his wife's mental health problems and bad ways, his children wouldn't have survived there. He had left his children with her and accepted that even though they were with Gerhard, they would be safe while he got himself prepared to bring them to his home as a single parent and start over.

He hoped he would survive, even though he was tired and bleeding and the cold was too much. Why would God make this world so cold? His teeth were chattering as he looked up. The sky was so dark, and where the stars should be, he could only see flakes of snow. It was a perfect night, 3 a.m. in the country, with no streetlights to block his view of the sky. He remembered his childhood in northern Mexico with the endless skies and really missed the mountains. They'd brought him peace on days when there was no hope. Life hadn't been easy there either. He'd worked hard alongside his vati, Jacob, and his brothers to turn the dusty soil to something that would nourish crops and feed their bodies. Some years, the crops died as soon as they were buried in the red dirt. Other years, it rained so hard that the water ran off the soil and never soaked in enough to help make anything grow. He now knew what it was like for Jacob to know he wouldn't be able to feed his family or help the community. When George had packed up his family and moved to Ontario, he'd had dreams of making a life there that would make his vati proud. He'd had dreams of many

CHAPTER ONE: THE SHOOTING

beautiful children and was trying so hard to be the vati he should have been, could have been.

He could feel the pain of the gunshot wound with every breath and tried again to go over the events of the night, remembering the sharp pain in his back and the noise. It took him a few minutes to understand that he had been shot. Where had the gun come from? he wondered. Why would Gerhard do this to him? Mennonites didn't have guns. When did he get a gun? He realized he didn't know him like he thought he did. Why would Gerhard do this to his friend and family? This was what it felt like to die, he thought to himself. God damn it. Yes, he was using God's name in vain. He'd always known God wasn't fair and had left him behind on many days when he was trying to fit in, to work and live in his new community.

He tried to block out the pain by breathing slowly, but he felt so alone. He was afraid of dying alone on a side road in a country that wasn't home. He would miss out on so much in his life. He had tried so hard but still couldn't help his wife. What would become of her? Her family didn't know what to do.

He loved the smell of the air. Sometimes, in the desert, he would stay out late with his friends. They would feel the night air creep onto them as they watched the stars and listened to coyotes. He took a big breath in, and he moaned as a sharp pain stopped him. Where the hell was Marshy? He tried to slow down his breathing and let the shooting pain in his chest settle down. His breathing was shallower now, and he feared help wouldn't come in time. Tears welled up in his eyes as he thought about his thirty-two years slipping slowly away.

He could feel the snow on his cheek turn from cold to burning and then numbness. His blood was melting the snow beneath his chest and running into his armpit. He had been hurt before, but this was the worst, and he started to cry, thinking of his six children. He wanted to be a better vati than he was, but it didn't seem likely now that he would have the chance. He coughed and tasted blood in his mouth. His breath gurgled as he tried to regain control over his breathing, but it was too mixed with sobs and pain. He had to let go.

When he made up his mind to just let it all go, he became more relaxed. There was less cold and pain, and he could see things more clearly. He could focus on what he had to do. He knew the fight was over as he was floating, more peaceful. The pain in his chest seemed to lessen, and he was getting used to it. It had to end somehow, the madness of his marriage and his children being taken away; he just hadn't wanted it to be this way.

Marshy was in Reg's truck as they drove down the roads, trying to find the car. Marshy wasn't from the area, so they had to start at the bar and work their way back to possible routes since it was so snowy. It was 7:30, close to 8 in the morning by the time Marshy was able to figure out the route that he'd taken from the Wolf residence and find the road he'd left George and the car on. Panicking, he could see the car; George was sitting outside of it, even though he'd left him inside.

George was a dusky blue with snow covering his face and body when they found him. There was no sign of blood remaining, as the snow had covered it. Reg pulled over and slowly opened the door. He wasn't sure what to expect since he'd never seen a dead person before. Marshy felt sick again and walked toward the car. Reg pulled his coat up around his neck. He couldn't remember a night as cold as this one in such a long time.

Marshy got to George first. He held his hands tight in his pant pockets, and he looked closely at George. He was hoping he would open his eyes and this would have been a big joke. Reg followed behind him and bent down to touch him. He could feel the cold of George's body on his fingertips as he checked his neck for a pulse. There was nothing except the beat of his own heart in his fingertips. Marshy was pacing now behind him, mumbling under his breath. He kneeled in front of the body and tried to lift George's arms, but they were stiff from cold or rigor mortis. Either way, it made him gasp. Reg took a breath and said, "We'd better call the police." Reg headed back to the pay phone in Port Burwell to make the call. George would sit with the dusting of snow on his face and eyelashes as he waited.

The sun was just starting to come up, and Ron had been driving around with the OPP in the blizzard looking for George's car. His radio buzzed as Tillsonburg dispatch called, telling him that they had received a call from someone in Port Burwell. The man stated that he had the driver of a car that knew where George

17

CHAPTER ONE: THE SHOOTING

was, and that they had found him. He said that he was dead outside the car and gave directions to his body. "The car is on the north end of the Woodworth sideroad." Ron went directly to the vehicle as the wind had died down. It was a bright sunrise, and he found George sitting straight up in the snow outside of the vehicle with his back leaning up against the outside edge of the passenger seat. The passenger door was wide open, and Ron could see that there were beer bottles outside of the car and some empties inside. Ron requested an ambulance and took charge of George's body, as was required of him, to make sure that any evidence that may be available stayed with the body right up until it was turned over to the coroner in Tillsonburg Hospital.

…

CHAPTER TWO:
THE LAST CHRISTMAS

1971

Anna was a pretty, dark-haired woman with porcelain white skin and dark brown eyes. She was slower than some in learning to read and count. Her parents reminded her that her role wasn't to worry about the written word, it was to have children and to be a good servant to God. She didn't do well in school, and her parents were quick to pull her out and keep her at home. They had to pay the Mennonite teacher at the school, so it would save time and money if Anna was able to stay home. She had worked hard with her mutti to learn what she would need to be a good wife. She had a shy smile and kept her long brown hair wrapped in a pretty scarf. She continued that Mennonite practice in Ontario, even though other things had been left behind in Mexico.

She was a woman who always had a hard time fitting in and, even as a child in Mexico, was not the best cook or mutti. She knew that when George married her, it was to save face in the community. Anna had been visiting George in the barns in Mexico where her brother worked, and they had been caught alone, talking. Mennonite girls couldn't be alone with men without ruining their name and possibly bringing shame to the family. Anna's vati, Johan, had found out and spoke with George's vati, and then there was pressure for the two of them to be married. Their marriage hadn't been about love; it had been about pride.

Now, in Canada, Anna had no sisters close by. She and George had settled into a place so small that it was referred to as a "blink of a town." It rested on the

CHAPTER TWO: THE LAST CHRISTMAS

Big Otter Creek and was famously known as the birthplace of Thomas Edison's grandparents. Thomas Edison was a famous inventor, and his remarkable inventions included the light bulb. It seemed ironic that Anna would also one day discover her own light bulb in this town of Vienna.

Otter Creek provided a waterway for lumber to travel to Lake Erie and beyond many years ago. Mennonites and migrant farmworkers came to the area because it had rich sandy loam soil, which grew many vegetables, tobacco, flowers, and crops. Finding enough workers to harvest crops was a challenge, and many travelled from Honduras and Mexico to work as seasonal migrant workers, earning extra money to have a better life in their home countries. This was how George and Anna had come to return to this area of the province. They had been there before as migrant workers, working in the fields and harvesting crops with their children.

Many of Anna and George's family had stayed in Mexico because they didn't have the courage to face another country or language and the title of *Kanadiar*, which was given to Mennonites that were exposed to Canadian ways of life. Often, Kanadiars weren't allowed back into the colony because the taste of a life of luxury in Ontario was seen as bringing sin into the community. The Bergthal and Chortizer Mennonites who had moved to northern Mexico and established the Manitoba Colony were one of the most conservative groups in Manitoba, and the elders and pastor had made the choice to live segregated to keep their devotion to the New Testament teaching.

Anna didn't have a car and couldn't read or write, so passing a test or understanding the road signs wasn't a solution to her isolation. They didn't have a horse or buggy for her to use in Ontario. It would take money to afford animals, feed, and a barn to house them. So far, that wasn't in the plans for their new home in Ontario. They had bought a car for the trip from Mexico to Canada, but George used it to get to his jobs. He was a quick learner and had gotten an Ontario driver's license and was able to find his way around and learn the names of people and towns. She, on the other hand, had no other Mennonites living close by in the community for her to visit or get support from. The Mennonite Central Committee had helped them settle into jobs and helped them find basic furnishings for their home, but there were no other families settled into the community that she knew. She had learned as a child to make cheese and butter, milk cows, feed chickens, and gather eggs. Here, she had nothing.

The rental home was arranged by a local farmer who was asked to provide housing for migrant workers for the area and he had a vacant home on one of his farms. The house was situated on a gravel side road and had a small grass yard with no barns or outbuildings for keeping animals. The house was better than other homes she had lived in, but she had never had a winter in Ontario to understand what she should be looking for in a house. They didn't have a choice in homes and took what they were given. The house was a former schoolhouse with grey insul-brick siding and a single peaked roof. At the front of the schoolhouse was a wooden vestibule with two doors that entered into a single hallway. Wooden signs appeared above each door reading Girls and Boys. On windy days, the shingles blew off the roof to the ground, exposing lumber to the elements. They had no shingles in Mexico, just thatch grass, so this was an unknown problem for them.

The front door was central, with a window on each side like eyes watching the road. There were three steps made of wood that creaked and gave way slightly under the weight of their feet before leading to the front door. Tall maple trees were around the house, a delight to see in the fall when the leaves had all turned. The family had never seen so much colour. Now, they stood like soldiers in the yard, stiff and providing only squeaking sounds as they rubbed on themselves during a winter storm. Through the front door, you walked through a short hallway until you reached a door leading to a large room with rusty tin ceilings that towered twelve feet over the floor. On each side of the door when you entered the home was a two-piece bath, one labelled Boys and the other Girls. There were drop toilets or pit latrines in the rooms, but at least you didn't have to go outside to use the washroom. When you looked into the house, you could see a short wall separating the large area into two separate rooms. The wall to the left had four kitchen cabinets, a white wooden hutch, and a gas stove. It also had a sink but no running water to use. The pump well was located in the backyard of the house. The kitchen had a single lightbulb that hung from the high ceilings, and when the front door was open, the breeze would move it from side to side, casting shadows on the chalkboard walls and tin ceilings.

The floors were made of wood, and many boards were broken to the point where you could see through to the dirt floor beneath the building. As you walked from the first room, there was a smaller room that held two beds. The remainder of the house was another big room, and that was where the rest of

CHAPTER TWO: THE LAST CHRISTMAS

beds were placed. A large pile of used clothing lay in the middle of the room on the floor for easy access. The schoolhouse had three windows on each side wall, giving good light into the house, for its four hanging lightbulbs were barely enough to light the home in the evenings. It was a bigger home than they had in Mexico, but it wasn't made of adobe and dirt. This was damp and rotting, and it seemed impossible to keep clean or warm.

She had a home that was falling apart and six children who needed something all the time. When George worked long hours, Anna would walk into town with the children to get groceries. Vienna was a one-street town. It was about a two-mile walk into town, which wasn't uncommon in Mexico where Anna had lived. She was used to walking farther than this for a store to buy flour or get fabric. The street had more stores than Anna and her children had ever had access to in their lives. As they walked toward town, they passed the public school. The kids weren't in school, and there were no plans to enrol them. Anna didn't feel that her children needed to go to school. She didn't understand taxes, and her parents and grandparents before her didn't send children to public education, so she wasn't about to start. Anna was suspicious of education in the public system based on stories from her parents and grandparents on what subjects students were being taught.

They turned to walk down Oak Street. The Vienna Hotel was on the right-hand side with a gas station straight ahead. Turning to the left, you could hear the hammering and snapping of welders from the Pace Welding shop. Next to them was Kay's Café and the Bugler's Grocery Store. A bit farther down the street, you would find Brown's Hardware store and Brown's Grocery store. Mike ran a meat market and butcher shop right beside Smyth's Barber Shop and Pool Room. Farther down the street was a general store/clothing store that stood on the corner of Edison Drive. With additional people in the summer, including migrant workers from other communities in Ontario, the streets were full, and the businesses were all busy and provided everything you needed without going to a bigger village.

When Anna and her children walked into town, she could feel people staring at her. She was still only wearing dresses when she could find them but soon stopped wearing her traditional pleated dresses and aprons, as she wanted to fit in. They would all walk in a row to town, and many people in the village had not seen a family with so many children in tow. When Anna and George were in town together, he would make her keep quiet when she was out because she spoke whatever thoughts came into her head, and it wasn't in English. She mumbled a lot to herself, often with personal put-downs or judgements she felt others were putting on her as she walked past them.

Learning English was a challenge, as she only spoke to her children and husband. They hadn't become part of the church or community, so she was very isolated. Her brother Gerhard and his wife lived in Port Burwell and were part of the church, raising their children to be part of it too. Gerhard worked every day with people from Ontario and had a good mastery of English to help him do the work he was given at the nursery. The pastor had come from Manitoba to help set up the church as more families moved back from Mexico. He wanted to ensure they knew the word of God and weren't tempted by the lives that others were leading that would cause them to stray away from their faith and beliefs. Even though Mennonites liked to be isolated from the general public, this was more than Anna could cope with, since she had no support system.

During her marriage, she had learned to be quiet when her husband was around. He would often shake his head in disgust when she offered her thoughts or ideas. Anna had many thoughts, and often, they weren't easily understood by others. She knew the voices in her head were from God, so she wanted everyone to benefit from them. When she had come to Canada, there were fewer people to talk to about her voices and the power they had, so she talked to them on her own and sometimes shared her thoughts with George. George told her to stop listening to the voices, to try and fit in.

In Vienna, when she walked into town to the store, men would stop and look at her. Many of these men were farm labourers and worked in the tobacco fields or fish plants. Anna liked that men noticed her when she walked down the streets. She wasn't getting much attention from George since he was working two jobs and not coming home very often. He even stayed away at night, leading her to believe that there was another woman he was running around with. Anna decided that if he had another woman, she could have another man. Mennonite men could always have a woman on the side and stay married, and it wasn't frowned upon by the church elders. Women didn't have the same arrangement, but Anna couldn't understand why there should be a difference. Now, there were no church elders watching her, and this made her feel like the risk of not feeling lonely would be worth it.

CHAPTER TWO: THE LAST CHRISTMAS

She knew what men wanted. From a young age, Mennonite men in her campo had asked her for sex, and she wanted to be popular, so she had often agreed. The men knew what to do to stop babies from being conceived. They had instructed Anna on how to touch and rub them. The topic of birth control was forbidden in the colonies, but through the quiet sharing of information, men were able to make sure they didn't end up in trouble with the pastors and elders by getting a girl pregnant before marriage. They pressured Anna to perform oral sex for their pleasure, and she was willing most of the time, as she enjoyed attention from the men. She also knew from what the men told her that if she let a man put his penis inside her, she would have a baby, so she avoided that. Having babies was God's gift to her, and she could only have them with her husband. She had learned this by watching farm animals, as she could never discuss this with her mother or family.

Anna had been going uptown more often when George was away and had met a fellow on several occasions. He smiled at her, and she shyly smiled back. She loved any attention and time away from the children. It was too much to cope with, all the kids and the house. So when she could escape and be admired by another adult, she took the chance. She liked that they found her pretty, even though she couldn't understand what they were saying. She knew what these men wanted, and she wanted it too. She started bringing men to the house for sexual favours. This particular man was friendly and gave her all the attention she was seeking. He drove a nice truck and would run his hands through her hair. He gave her booze, and she longed for the taste of the alcohol to numb the sins she was committing. After the first man, another man came, and then another. Word got out in the migrant worker and farming community that, for the small price of a bottle of alcohol, you could have sexual favours with a Mennonite woman.

The kids were used to these men coming and going. When Anna brought a man home, they had sex in the bed in the small room that three of the boys shared. The kids would go outside and play and try to stay out of the way of the noise, laughter, and drinking. The men would usually come during the day or early evening. Sometimes, the repeat visitors would bring food that the kids would eat while Anna performed oral sex in the other room. There were many men who would come to the house and not bring a bottle of booze, and Anna would get angry at them. They would hit her, slap her across the face, and force her to perform sexual acts on them. She would feel sad and angry when they left. The children would see the bruises and blood from the assault and look cautiously at her. When there were many days with no drinks, Anna became more agitated. She would mumble more to herself and often hit the children. They soon learned that they could spend time outside, especially in the summer, and not have to face her frustrations and withdrawal from alcohol.

On this particular day, George came home between shifts to check on the house and bring some groceries. He saw all of the kids outside with short sleeves, some with shoes and others without. It was far too cold for them to be outside. He pulled up in his car and quickly got out. Anger built inside him as he noticed a truck in the laneway. His oldest boys were getting so big, it shocked George every time he saw them, and yet he was still trying to figure out his life.

"Where's your mutti?" he asked them. "Why are you outside and not in, where it's warm?"

The kids quickly explained that there was a man in the house and they had to stay outside. George was getting angrier as he processed what was going on. "Come with me. Let's get you warm and fed." He opened the door of the house and led them all inside.

Anna could hear the commotion in the next room, and so could the man she was with. Anna stopped and heard her husband's voice over those of the children. "You'd better get outta here. My husband is home." The man zipped up his pants, looking frantic. He peeked out the door to see George standing there.

"Who are you? Get the hell out of my house!" George took a step toward him, and he quickly darted for the door. George recognized him from the bar.

"What do you care?" Anna yelled to George from the other room. "You're never here. You're gone day and night. I'm lonely, and Gertruda is old enough to look after the kids now," she added in her defense as she straightened her clothing. Gertruda was the oldest of the six children although she was just eleven years old she knew when she needed to step up and take care of her siblings.

George clenched his fists and punched the wooden table. It broke in two, revealing Gertruda and Maria hiding under it. They only had one table, and they felt that hiding to escape another fight was the best solution. Anna, still dressing, yelled her defense at George as she started to understand how angry he really was this time. It wasn't the first time he'd found her with another man.

CHAPTER TWO: THE LAST CHRISTMAS

George started to get some food together for the children and heat the house. He needed a distraction to think over what was going on and how he could fix it. In his vati's house and in those of other Mennonite men, the man ruled the home, and the woman managed it. He had run out of ideas of how to help Anna to properly fill her role. So had her mutti and sisters. He set up the powdered milk and was heating water on the stove to prime the frozen well pump. There was no furnace in the house, so he started the oven and left the door open to heat the kitchen. He'd brought cereal and oatmeal for the kids. They would have hot oatmeal and warm by the oven door. Cautiously, they gathered around the stove for warmth as Anna sat in the other room, trying to figure out how to get out of this situation. Her voices had been loud, and she had tried to listen, but sometimes, it was hard.

You deserve to be loved. This is your house. He just thinks he can boss you around because you're his woman.

Anna was reaffirming her feelings with the support of her inner voices.

The children eagerly accepted the oatmeal and ate hungrily as George watched them. He knew that nothing he could say to Anna would help the situation. He had tried to discipline Anna and teach her right from wrong, but she wouldn't listen to him. Since coming back to Canada, he'd decided that he would have to try and get enough money together to get the children away from Anna to give them a better life.

The children all smiled at each other and talked. George spoke quietly to them. "There's more oatmeal if you need it, and I'll drop off bread later."

George had to leave for his night shift at the bar. He left the oven door open and arranged blankets on the floor to make sure the children were kept warm while sleeping.

Anna stayed in the other room. Her thoughts were racing on how to defend her actions and come out on top of the situation. In her head, she had made up the story of his violence and wanting to hurt her and the kids. As she ruminated on the facts and his lack of understanding of her need for physical and personal company, she became more convinced that she was in danger and decided to walk to her brother's house. He had always stuck up for her and was patient. His wife, Margaret, was always trying to keep Anna following the Bible and doing the reading for her, but Anna was getting tired of hearing her preaching all of the time. Gerhard was more understanding, and Anna knew how to get what she needed from him.

Gerhard, Margaret, and their children lived on the grounds of McConnell Nurseries. Gerhard and his children all worked at the nursery and arranged work for other migrant workers coming to the area. This was a big job for Gerhard, and having this home on the business property was a sign of prestige for him with the promise of a good life in Ontario. Gerhard was also closely tied to the Old Colony Mennonite Church elders and pastor. He wanted to be viewed as a prominent citizen in the church, one that would be able to lead the church in the future. He was able to send more money to the church and was becoming known as a more prosperous immigrant in the community and within his congregation. It was important to maintain this level of social standing for Gerhard, and he wouldn't allow anyone to tarnish his reputation and good name.

Anna put sweaters, hats, coats, and two layers of pants on each child. She knew that it was bitter outside, and she hated being cold. She went through her five-foot pile of clothing from various family and neighbours and was able to find enough shoes for everyone. She had all the clothes in a large pile, and each day, the children would go through it and find things to wear. It wasn't often they were washed. The baby, John, was just two, so he would need to be carried. She lined up the kids, put John on her back, and they started walking. It was about a five-mile walk in the knee-deep snow with cold winds blowing.

Anna walked. The other children tried to keep up, and the younger ones straggled behind. Eventually, Gertruda was carrying little Peter on her back too, as he was just three and having a hard time keeping up. There were occasional sobbing tears heard through the whistling winter gales and blowing snow, but they forged on. Anna could be very stubborn, and the more she walked, the more she wrote a story inside her head about how much of a victim she was in this marriage and life. She wouldn't tell her brother and his wife the real reasons for George's anger. She wanted to them to think she was innocent. As she walked, she listened to the voices in her head, and they were switching things around in her story for her.

George was at fault. He forced those men to come to you for sex so he could have alcohol and money, and then he wouldn't give you any.

CHAPTER TWO: THE LAST CHRISTMAS

Anna heard this, knowing that her brother would help her if he knew this was going on. She thanked the voice in her head for giving her the answer she needed.

It was 8 p.m. when they arrived at Gerhard and Margaret's door. Anna was out of breath. She was fit, but it was a long walk, and the baby John was covered in snow with ice hanging from his hair when the door opened. They were welcomed into the warm home, even though everyone was surprised about their journey.

"Where's George? What are you doing with the kids out at night?" asked her brother, Gerhard. His wife was taking the children into the living room to warm them.

Anna told stories of George's anger and his drunken behaviour, the forced sex with strange men, and Gerhard became panicked. How would the church see this, his own sister and brother-in-law doing these vile acts of disobedience to the word of God? She talked about him staying out at night, running around behind her back and not coming home. He didn't provide for the children, and she had begun to fear for their lives. She felt threatened by her husband and feared he might hurt her. She showed him her bruises to add to her story from the encounters with the strange men that she had been having to the house. These were the words that would stick in Gerhard's head as he tried to come up with next steps while still keeping his job and prominent standing in the church.

Gerhard felt responsibility for his sister and her children. His wife, Margaret, made warm milk for the kids and heated up some leftover soup and buns. They ate greedily, and then their cousins took them all upstairs to find a place for them to sleep. There weren't enough blankets for everyone, so the smaller children shared some and curled up together to get warm.

When Anna was done describing her scenario, she felt emotionally and physically drained. Before the kids were asleep, Anna had made her bed on a mattress on the floor upstairs and was fast asleep. She was warm and safe.

The next week was Christmas. The house was chaos with both families together and their twelve children running around. Gerhard was working, and Margaret was trying to keep the house going and the kids cared for. Anna wasn't up early to help, completely uninterested in baking bread or cooking. Margaret pushed her to participate, as there wasn't enough food for everyone.

George returned home the next morning to find it empty, with the stove door open as he had left it. He went to Gerhard's and asked if Anna was there. Gerhard was defensive and protective. "You can't be treating women like you do, George, hitting them and yelling. Anna told me what you're like when you come from work, drunk and wanting to hurt her and the kids."

George listened but quickly defended himself. "Did she tell you why I was angry? She had a man in the house for sex while the kids were outside, cold and hungry. She was getting bottles of booze for sexual favours."

Gerhard was taken aback. He recalled the conversation he'd had with his sister and felt anger building inside him. "You're telling lies. You're a drunk who runs around on his wife and won't take care of his kids. You get out of here. We'll find a way to help her and your kids. I hear from people who go to the bar that you have a girlfriend. You run around with her while Anna is at home, trying to look after the kids with no money or food. She's not well enough for that."

"I can look after my kids. I just need her to stop bringing strangers into the house and focus on caring for the children when I'm away. I work long hours to make sure I have enough money for all of them. She just uses it for buying booze."

Gerhard turned his back on George, shaking his head. "You're telling lies. Anna needs more help that you can provide, and we can help her here."

He shut the door, and George walked to his car to drive to work. Gerhard had known all about Anna even before George had married her. He'd known that she wasn't a fast learner and that in order to make friends, she did things with men that a Christian woman shouldn't do. In Ontario, Gerhard had heard about the things she had done in the colony, and he knew from the migrant workers in the area what she was doing in her home in Vienna. He'd discredited the stories to provide some distance between his sister's family and his own. His reputation was at risk if people believed the stories to be true. He also knew the pressure that George had been under to marry Anna, and that George's duty in the eyes of God was to stay married to her.

George was frustrated but grateful for his job and coworkers. They took his mind off of his problems. He had met a woman named Tootsie at work who he had grown to respect and trust. She looked at him like no other woman had ever before. She was kind, and she worked hard to look after her kids. He could feel

CHAPTER TWO: THE LAST CHRISTMAS

his heart warm around her. He could see himself making plans with her, and often, she would help him find ways to move forward with his life in Ontario. She gave him hope and love, something he hadn't had in most of his life. His relationship with her had grown over the past few months, as he was working longer hours and was therefore able to share some of his fears for his children and the things they were being exposed to. She would listen and help him find a way out of the situation. He knew the holidays were coming up, and he wanted it to be different this year for his family. Even though his children were at his brother-in-law's, he felt that they were safe there, that Anna wouldn't be having men in the house or exposing his children to them.

Tootsie and George had decided to go out shopping for gifts. He had only a week now until the 25th, so he needed her help to know what was suitable as gifts for his children. He remembered, as a child, how important and exciting Christmas had been. His family never had any money for gifts, but they still celebrated with food and treats. He prepared each gift for his children along with a bowl of hard candies and an orange.

At the end of his shift on Christmas Eve, he went to Gerhard's to see the children and give them their gifts for Christmas. Gerhard and Margaret willingly let him in the house. He watched with a smile on his face as his six children enjoyed their dolls and trucks. The boys got trucks and were pleased. The girls each got a doll in a purple dress. It had blonde hair and eyes that closed when she lay down. They all looked so happy. It broke his heart to think of what they had been going through over the past few years, but things were changing.

George had enough money saved up to get a new place. He was going to get the kids away from Anna and give them a good start. It wouldn't be easy, but it would make life better. He left that Christmas satisfied that he had done something good for his children.

Anna was nowhere to be seen at the house. She often hid when she was afraid or in trouble. She knew the stories she told her brother weren't true and didn't want to get caught. But George didn't care. He knew, moving forward, that his life wouldn't include her. He had seen what a better woman and life could do to make him feel stronger. He knew that people in the community respected him, and he was going to work hard and get ahead. Time was what he needed, and yet he felt like he didn't have enough of it. He felt an urgency to get things going.

CHAPTER THREE:
ANNA'S CHILDHOOD IN MEXICO

1920s

Anna was part of the first generation of Mennonites in her family to be born in Mexico. Her parents, Johan and Maria, had boarded the train in Plum Coulee, Manitoba with their community and travelled across North America to a border city in Mexico called Juárez. There, they had chartered thirty-six trains and travelled for eight days. When they arrived, the Mexican government greeted them and also provided a group of soldiers with rifles and revolvers to travel with them on the train and prevent them from being robbed while travelling to their final destination of San Antonio de los Arneales. The main industry in the region was the silver mines, some farming, and a total of thirteen trees. The journey's backdrop was the Sierra Madre Occidental mountains and red soil blowing in the wind from the steam train as they passed.

When the Manitoba Mennonites arrived, there were already Germans from Russia living in northern Mexico and areas to the south of Mexico. They had come after WW1, expecting more prosperity and wealth, and many had found it there by setting up industry, stores, and factories. They had set up a few shops and were able to translate for the Mennonites, as they could also speak Spanish. The Mennonites in Chortitza, Manitoba had sent a delegation to assess the land and negotiate with the government to secure it for them.

CHAPTER THREE: ANNA'S CHILDHOOD IN MEXICO

The Manitoba Mennonites arrived with corn, firewood, hogs, horses, cows, and cooking items on the train. What wasn't stolen by the Mexicans was used to plant the first crop and build their homes. They would learn from failed crops in the first few years that they needed to change from the wheat they were planting to find a different way to success. The excitement was visible on the group's faces as they smiled and thought of the farms they could establish to begin their colony. After the Manitoba Mennonites arrived and the area became more populated, there were enough people in the village to qualify it as a town, and it was named Cuauhtémoc. They began setting up the colony the same as they had in Canada and Russia. It was hard to use the normal community names as Mexicans would not be able to pronounce them, so they decided to change them to campos and number them so that there was a way for outsiders to understand the layout and how to reach certain regions. Each campo was a village on its own, with shops and churches.

The Mennonites had bought over two hundred thousand acres of land to begin their new community. They watched the Mexicans plant their fields and soon changed to a more sustainable method. Some of the Mennonites experimented with methods to increase crop yields. They would scrape the dry dirt off the land, and using a sharp stick, they would put a seed in each hole. It was labour-intensive, and the children would help ensure each seed was in its bed to grow and not wash away with each rain. They would do this for over fifty acres of land. Windmills would be erected to pump water to help crops grow. It took time to learn the methods of success in this new land and to build the perseverance to last through droughts, starvation, and tests by God to follow the ways of their leaders.

When Mexico agreed to allow the Mennonites from Manitoba to immigrate to their country, they were pleased to welcome the diversity of culture and begin building the mestizo race. At the same time, Mormons were also arriving on their own parcels of land. The Mexicans welcomed immigrants, particularly those of European descent who would bring fair skin, blonde hair, and blue eyes, helping the local population shed their characteristic dark skin, hair, and eyes for a more merged look. There was some discussion within the government that the lack of ethnic diversity in Mexico might have been the cause of some of the discord within the country.

All Mennonites were registered with the government, and a method of assessing racial features was developed to help them work toward building a more robust population. Their registration cards contained information such as: race, colour of eyes, shape of nose, and general appearance, including cranial shape. The practice of using eugenics was common in immigration screening to ensure that Mennonites allowed into Mexico possessed the right characteristics to enhance the population and improve the diversity of the region. However, the thought that Mennonites and Europeans would transform their population were soon rejected as it became obvious that the Mormons and Mennonites stayed within their own groups to marry and have children.

Mennonites had an excellent reputation as hard workers who could turn unusable land into farmland. Overall, the Mexicans saw them as a good economic boost to the region. At the same time that Mennonites were granted land, Mormons also arrived and settled into another region separate from them. The beliefs of the Mormons and Mennonites were alike in that they both wanted privacy, no rules from governments, and were all patriarchal communities.

This upbringing and the cultural expectation to stay within your own community for marriage was how Anna was raised and how her church expected any congregation member to behave. Anna would have spoken Plautdietsch, also known as Low German, in her home and German in church. English had not been widely used as a method of communicating. The Mexican government would encourage the Mennonites to learn Spanish, and many men did. For women, it wasn't as prevalent, as they couldn't speak directly to Mexicans at markets or shops without their husbands beside them. That isn't to say that many women didn't know Spanish—many were in fact able to understand the market negotiations and discussions between the native Mexicans and their husbands and sons. After years of failed crops, many families couldn't afford to send their children to the Mennonite schools and would instead send them to Mexican schools, which were free. This was frowned upon by the leaders, and often, these families would not be allowed to remain part of the colonies.

Anna had never known any other life but could still imagine better. She loved watching the daily rituals of life in Cuauhtémoc; she had seen the natives at the market wearing colourful clothes, dancing and laughing with their children and partners. She knew what uninhibited joy looked like, and it was very different from her life in the campo. She had been raised speaking German, Plautdietsch, and a bit

CHAPTER THREE: ANNA'S CHILDHOOD IN MEXICO

of Spanish. She knew that her life was full of struggle just as her parents' and grandparents' lives had been, but she was taught through her congregation that suffering for your beliefs was an honourable act that should be worn with pride. She had been taught that from suffering comes devotion and that God only gives you what you are able to bear. She believed that if she worked hard, He would provide, and so Anna laboured hard with her family. Her mutti would often say that being together made it seem like they never suffered alone. Women in their campo learned to keep their thoughts to themselves from an early age. Their female voices were meant to be heard in pleasant, nurturing tones, and their thoughts must mirror their husband's, vati's, or pastor's.

As a teenage woman in the Mennonite colony, Anna had already learned her place. The *weibsleit*, female folk, knew their lives were this way because God created the *mannsleit*, male folk, first. When He created Adam first, He meant for men to walk ahead and lead, and women would sit and walk behind their husbands, yet support and stand beside them. There was no room in their interpretation of the Bible for women to have individual thoughts or share them outside the home. Some husbands ensured that they were not shared in the home either.

Anna's predecessors were ultraconservative, which was why they kept moving through Europe, Prussia, Manitoba, and then to Mexico. They wanted to live the purest life possible and remove all influences from the world to ensure that they could maintain their pure life. Women had to talk to each other secretly when they needed support. Women carried the load of child-rearing, home maintenance, cooking, and cleaning on their own. They also would do the chores and help in the fields if needed. The weibsleit learned at a young age that their voices were to be used in singing and praising their vatis, husbands, and brothers and not condemning or judging them or their actions.

Anna's favourite part of the day was watching the sun rise in the morning. The mountains in the background shadowed her daily chores. They could change colours in front of her eyes. Sometimes, as she hung out her family's clothes on the line, the mountains were a burned red and orange. Other times, they were purple and exotic. The clouds could be seen for miles overhead, their shapes fascinating Anna as she wondered if they would bring rain or just drift past to the next colony or state in Mexico. Some Mennonites in the village frowned upon Anna's parents for allowing the children to play in the mountains and hike the trails because they believed the children should be working harder so they would be more successful.

Anna's mutti had her nerves to manage, and some days, she was in bed all day. Despite the sun shining in the windows, her mutti would lay in darkness without the energy to do her morning chores or duties.

Anna enjoyed her moments of walking in the desert and looking at the mountains. In the Mennonite teachings, it was known that "less idle time means more food on the table." This echoed in Anna's ears, but when she got to be free of chores and just walk, she considered it a reward for working hard and living a life of Godliness.

Anna accepted the life that her parents struggled every day to maintain and develop. She was one of ten children. Her mutti, Maria, delivered thirteen children in total, three dying during birth or shortly after. When Maria started having her babies in Mexico, she hadn't had midwives near her, so she was forced to give birth at home on her own. A campo experienced Mennonite woman was called to come and help, but in the end, it hadn't been enough to save them all.

Anna had four brothers named Heinrich before the fourth one would live to hold the name. Naming of babies in the Mennonite families was respectfully done by tradition. The firstborn daughter was traditionally named after her vati's mutti. The firstborn son was named after his vati's vati. The secondborn daughter was named after her vati's mutti, and the secondborn son was named after his mutti's vati. The rest were named after the husband's siblings from oldest to youngest. If a child died, the name would be reused to ensure tradition was upheld until a child lived.

On this Monday, the race was on to see who could get their laundry out first after a day of rest. Anna heard her mutti put the water to boil on the stove for the wash around 4:30 in the morning. Anna lay in bed in the darkness and listened to life in their adobe home. There was no electricity, so her room was only lit from the oil lights in the kitchen casting shadows across the walls. Her vati, Johan, and her brothers were up to milk the cows and then to work on the neighbour's farm hoeing beans. It was only her parents and younger sister living at home now, as her brother and sisters had their own homes and families. Anna lay in bed a short while and heard talking and the shuffling of feet. No one made any attempt to stay quiet to let Anna sleep. She was the last one up.

CHAPTER THREE: ANNA'S CHILDHOOD IN MEXICO

Anna shared a room with her younger sister, Agatha. As Anna heard the house coming alive, she said to herself, "I'll lay here just a bit longer." The ceilings and walls were a crisp white from the whitewashing, and the shadows formed shapes across the ceiling that looked like birds flying overhead. Nothing pleased Mutti more than clean, white walls in a land of red dirt and the smell of Pine-Sol cleaner. Anna could feel the wind blow into her room from the open windows with a hotness that predicted the type of day ahead.

Anna jumped to her feet in her floor-length nightgown and pulled it over her head to get dressed. She had some favourite dresses, but it was a workday, so a workday dress it was. She stepped into the dark burgundy dress and pulled it over her hips, reaching back to button the neck. Anna really liked the simplicity of the dress and the crisp pleats in the front. When she dressed this way, she felt pure in the eyes of the colony and God. She didn't own any shoes, as her feet were still growing. It wasn't uncommon for children to never own shoes and only start wearing them when they were married and grown-up.

Reaching up to her hair, already braided, she fixed any loose hair into the braids with pins. Anna had fine, black hair, but she preferred blonde. Everyone in Mexico had black hair, but those with blonde hair stood out as special. Anna picked a white embroidered scarf and wrapped it over her head and under her chin. The wind was blowing, and red dirt would be everywhere, but she wouldn't let it get in her hair. Anna liked that her hair was getting long. She knew that she wasn't allowed to cut it. The church felt that a woman cutting hair showed vanity, and they didn't want that. Men liked to be sure that women were as God created them, and any adding of fancy hairpins or nylons would be judged. No woman wanted to be judged while she was trying to find a husband, and that was exactly what Anna was trying to do. She wanted to blend in and be perfect in the eyes of the elders and God. Anna was trying very hard to be perfect. She finished dressing and went to help with the laundry.

"It's about time you're up. Your little sister is already out doing the chores. Grab some bread and jam and then help me with the wash," said Mutti. She spoke in Plautdietsch to Anna, who recognized the urgency in her tone. She could eat her bread while putting clothes through the wringer. With a smaller family at home now, there really was no excuse to not have the wash out first.

Anna grabbed a slice of bread with home-churned butter and stood next to the machine. She looked at her mutti, bent over the washbasin with the scrubboard, scrubbing with soap on the white undershirts. Her mutti worked and never complained. She was a pretty woman, with dark eyes and hair. She had few grey hairs despite her worries and work. Her mutti always did her part to make sure her husband was able to do his. They were a team. She read the Bible each day to make sure she was living according to His word. She enjoyed the women in the community and had a few close friends, despite the distance between farms.

She could find joy in all the daily work, Anna thought to herself. She wished she could be just like her when she became a wife and mutti. As she was thinking, her mutti looked up. "Anna, get working and stop dreaming. We need to get the wash out before Gertruda next door." Anna smiled. She enjoyed the competition and started to run the clothing through the wooden and steel wringer, pulling heavily on the clothes while frantically cranking the steel handle to squeeze the water from each item. They were very fortunate to have a wringer to use, as many families just wrung out the clothes by hand and put them on the line. It was hard work scrubbing, and Anna, her mutti, and her sister had broad, muscular shoulders because of this.

As Anna finished one item, her mutti handed her the next. Her mutti had the boiled water in the steel tub with the washboard and worked rhythmically up and down the corrugated metal to scrub the dirt from the clothes. When she was finished, Anna picked up her basket of clothing and walked outside to the clothesline, her mutti following. They walked briskly to the line to get the first pair of overalls out. Now, with only her father at home, there were just his overalls to hang out. Her mutti started, grabbing the top pair of pants from the laundry pile, and sped up to get the clothespin bag. She had her damp cloth to clean the line as she hung out the clothes. Red dust from the soil would leave marks on her whitewash, and she wasn't going to be judged because of that. She hung them from the suspenders one after the other. Anna checked over her shoulder to see if anyone else was out. Some homes were just coming out with their wash. Her mutti sped up with a smile forming on her face, making the wrinkles around her eyes more noticeable. Next were the blue work shirts, pinned from the bottom to keep the clothespin pleats from the shoulders, followed by the girls' dresses. A woman's worth was measured in the speed, whiteness, and tidiness of the clothes on the line. She'd won that day. It would be talked about at Bible reading that they were the first that Monday.

CHAPTER THREE: ANNA'S CHILDHOOD IN MEXICO

By 7 a.m., all the morning work had been completed, and it was time to slow things down a bit. Anna looked out to see Agatha coming in from the barn with colour in her cheeks from the heat. It was going to be another very hot day. Agatha carried the daily eggs and milk and walked through the open front door into the house. She laid the eggs and milk on the table and started assembling the ingredients on the wooden table for bread. She tossed flour on the surface for rolling. It was like lining up for church; everyone knew what to do and how to do it without saying many words. Maria enjoyed this time alone with her girls, and she really enjoyed the silence. She found peace in doing the daily tasks, and with only two girls home now, she had more time for needlework and quilting. Anna, on the other hand, didn't enjoy the silence and was bursting to talk. She had given her mutti enough peace this morning.

Maria pointed in the corner at the broom so Anna could begin sweeping. The previous day left crumbs and manure on the dirt floors. Every day, and sometimes twice a day, the dirt floors were swept and sprayed with water to keep the dust down. Maria had memories of the painted wooden floors in her parents' home in Manitoba. She remembered how easy they were to polish and clean and how much joy her mother had in painting them. Someday, there would be wooden floors in her house again. She just had to be patient. Anna started in the corner and worked her way across the room with her corn broom.

"What are you smiling about this morning, Agatha?" asked Maria.

Anna stopped to look at her sister as she finished sweeping and started mixing the flour and eggs for *tweebak*, bread. Agatha started to speak. "I really like Johan. He's so tall and handsome. He has the shiniest black hair and strongest back," she said, blushing. "He nodded at me today when I was done the milking."

Anna watched her sister. Johan was the brother of a boy she really liked. How could her sister be younger and already planning her husband? She knew that often in the campos, brothers married sisters from a neighbouring campo, but she felt like she needed to be more special than her own little sister. She looked at Agatha with critical eyes. She was shorter than Anna, heavier, and didn't press her dresses or embroider as well as Anna.

"You will make an awful wife, Agatha. You don't even know how to keep a house," said Anna. Agatha looked at Anna, startled by the words.

"Anna, you don't speak like that to your sister," said Mutti. "You're talking from jealousy and envy, and that's not wanted here. You be kind." Maria let out a big sigh. Was there to be no peace today with Anna? She could be so challenging. So often, Maria prayed to God for strength in helping Anna see the way of God. She also knew that since Anna was a slow learner, it would take longer and require more patience than she currently had.

Anna was red-faced with anger. She didn't think her words were harsh enough. She wanted a courtship and wedding first. She was older. Agatha looked at the table and listened to her mutti scold Anna.

"Agatha, have you talked with Johan at all at church?"

Agatha had a gentle smile. "I have, and he seems very nice."

Maria smiled. She remembered young love. She knew that Agatha would be a good wife for any man. She was kind and gentle and would raise her family in the fellowship of God and the rules of the colony. She turned her head to see Anna looking at her sister with a clenched jaw. "Anna, you like George, Johan's brother, right? Maybe you can both marry a Peters boy." Agatha looked timidly toward her sister in the hope that she would be smiling. Anna looked at both of them and nodded. She wasn't sure about this family marriage thing. She felt that no matter what, her sister would get more attention than she would.

Agatha knew that Anna would get her revenge later and feared what it might look like. Anna had bad moods, and lately, she had them almost every day. She could be so sweet one minute and then have the hatred of Satan in her voice and eyes in the next. Agatha knew that Anna wanted to be married and would let her have her time.

Since birth, Anna had had a more difficult time reading and fitting in than her siblings. Her sisters were old enough that they didn't want to take time out for her, and her parents sometimes referred to her as "a bit slow." Their expectations of her were different from her sisters. She had the gift of hearing voices at a young age, and most of the time, they told her to do good things. She told her mutti about the voices, and the clergy and other leaders also knew. Telling everyone would ensure that people understood that Anna might not always act as she should in the community, and hopefully, they wouldn't judge her as quickly. They would pray for Anna's voices to stop and hope that God would help her live her best life in the colony.

She tried to read the Bible, but the words wouldn't stay on the page. "Blessed are the meek" would become "Meek the are blessed." She might have needed glasses, but in the colonies, they were expensive. Besides, she could see well

CHAPTER THREE: ANNA'S CHILDHOOD IN MEXICO

enough to embroider, bake, and do her chores, so there would be no money spent on glasses.

In addition, she'd had a quick temper since she'd hit puberty. She verbally retaliated against any comments made about her that held the slightest criticism. This wasn't how a Mennonite woman should have acted in the home or in the community.

Anna knew that her sisters had it easier than her, but she was just as pretty. She was certain she might not have been as smart as the average girl in the colony at school, but she was finished school now. She could focus on sewing and embroidery and learning how to keep a good house and eventually have children to care for.

Anna was still ruminating about Agatha liking George's brother as she kneaded the dough. George had three brothers, so it wasn't a surprise that they might marry into the family twice. All were handsome, tall, and good farmworkers. Anna knew that any future husbands would have to come from the colonies; she was only allowed to marry another Mennonite. Anna wanted to be married by the time she was eighteen or nineteen. That was her personal goal. Even though she was a bit slow, her parents would make sure that she had the skills needed to keep a man and home. She knew that even if she was slow, God would give her children. It would be her gift for having more struggles than others had. Anna knew her role in life was to make babies, but they came from God and not from her. From the hair on her head to the socks on her feet, Anna's existence was managed by God and the men in the church and colony.

In the hours after church on a Sunday, before *faspa* (a light meal) and evening church service, she would sometimes sit with her teenage cousins and neighbours and eat *knacksot*, sunflower seeds, and drink homemade *spiatess*, alcohol. The grownups didn't know about the drink the teens were mixing, but they had also secretly been making alcoholic drinks for years. The youth learned it from their parents, after all. The church leaders wouldn't approve. Anna and her friends would talk about boys and girls and spit out the seeds from the *knacksot* into the red dirt under the evening skies as they sipped. These were the moments where there were no rules, and children could dream of their own homes, families, and the work they might have wanted to do like mechanics and quilting.

NOT MY KIND OF MENNONITE

Jacob and Maria Peters. Anna is the child holding the apron in front of their Mexican home.

CHAPTER FOUR:
GEORGE'S CHILDHOOD IN MEXICO

1920s

George loved living in the desert, waking in the early hours of the morning to see the sun rising over the mountains. From his farmyard, he could look across the vast space and see red and purple mountains. They symbolized freedom for him. It wasn't often that he got to go horseback riding there, but he really enjoyed the wind in his hair and being free of responsibilities and his family. At the age of fifteen, George knew his role in the family and community. George took great pride in his work on the farm and helping his vati, but he thrived on silence. He could think, dream, and just listen to the world around him.

George's vati, Jacob Peters, had been one of the early settlers to Chihuahua. His family had bought their parcel of land of one hundred and sixty acres, and they shared a barn for their animals with the farm next door. They grew corn and beans. They needed to have a few cows for milk and meat, as well as horses for their buggies and transportation. But farming was more difficult than expected. The pastures were drying up from drought and leaving their livestock thin. With no crop, there was no feed for the cattle or horses or themselves. Often, with the winds and downpours of rain, they had very poor crops. They didn't have the money that other farmers had for irrigation ditches and watering

CHAPTER FOUR: GEORGE'S CHILDHOOD IN MEXICO

systems. The one thing that Jacob was able to do in the community was go from farm to farm with his horse and wagon and pick up the milk jugs to take to the cheese factory. He was given a small sum of money for doing this, and it let him get away from the farm.

When the crops failed, Jacob became angry and was hard to please in any way. It caused him to reflect on his dedication to scripture and God and why he was being punished. He found it hard to accept he was less of a farmer, less of a Mennonite, than others, so he often had outbursts of anger when others asked how his crop yields were for the season.

Each campo had its own school. The teacher was always a man chosen from the colony with no specific training. A simple reader, the Bible, and hymnary were the basic study materials. Many settlers didn't believe Mexico would be their final home and impatiently waited for a sign from God on what to do next, especially after droughts and crop failure. George and his brothers would only sporadically attend school and learn to read only from the Bible in German because they needed their hands and backs working in the fields and barns.

Jacob would not approve of his "thinking." George was expected to listen to his father, the elders and not spend time trying to find alternatives or new solutions to problems that were already managed by the colony. He was a hard man who had struggled his entire life to compete with the other men in the colony for success. As a Mennonite, life was chosen for him at birth. All colony life took place under the eye of the church, and men in the community were responsible to raise their families to fit into the mold laid out.

George watched his vati at the colony meetings, stiff and formal in his responses to questions of diversification of property or business around the cheese factory. Jacob felt important and knew that even as other farmers were making more money than him and buying more animals and building more homes, he would eventually get what he worked for. It was important to him to be accepted and part of this group of founders. History was being made with their move to Mexico, and it was up to him to help his people prosper. His sons would learn this from him.

Jacob had been adopted at birth. He knew that he was looked down on by his relatives as being a bastard child, but he had been taken in and raised with the same faith and expectations. He was brought up with a firm hand and was smaller than most of his cousins in size.

George's vati taught him with the back of his hand how to work harder and longer. George didn't get to go to school very much, but he picked up a lot from the people at the markets, Mexicans, and others, so he could read and write German, Spanish, and a bit of English. He was good with his reading and numbers, but that wasn't what his vati wanted. Reading the Bible and singing hymns was what the pastors wanted. George was allowed to use his mind for repetitive religious verses but not for independent thinking and planning. It was best to stay as one of the flock than to wander with your mind and heart onto a different life.

George stood at six feet, five inches. He had blonde hair and blue eyes and was a perfect Mennonite in the dark-skinned land. He was the next generation to lead the colony, and Jacob wanted to make sure he understood this privilege and right and how to get what he deserved.

Jacob was short-tempered and had a heavy fist. George and his brothers knew this well. He had no patience for any women, especially his wife, Gertruda. She was to keep a good home. If she did her job, he could do his. Gertruda had a hard life looking after her four sons and husband. There were few women to meet with, as the farms were far apart. If she wanted to talk with other women, it would be at church, and that was just for a few hours. She lived in a world of making sure her Jacob was happy, or else she would pay the price with a beating.

One day, when the supper wasn't ready on time, Gertruda waited for the slap and punch from Jacob, which he delivered with a fierce scowl. She knew that one hit led to another hit, and then he would force himself onto her. Jacob hit Gertruda hard and knocked her to the floor. On this day, George's brother Johan stepped in to protect her and was met with a hit so hard that he lay unconscious on the ground. The rest of them watched, frozen in fear. She said nothing. George couldn't help his mutti up or get cold water compresses for her bruises. He had faced his own punishment many times after trying to defend his family and didn't have the strength to do it that day. Jacob always used his fists when he felt that others in the community were talking about him, his farming, his sons, or his wife. George knew his actions weren't right, but at the same time, it was how many of the men kept their wives in line and ran their houses.

George watched her struggle to see through her swelling eyes as she prepared their dinner and set it out for them. Often, Jacob would take an extra portion just so she wouldn't have any for her own dinner. She had to learn her lesson. He

CHAPTER FOUR: GEORGE'S CHILDHOOD IN MEXICO

taught his sons the same. Because Johan had tried to protect their mother, he was nowhere to be seen for dinner. George knew the anger that ran in his vati's blood was because God was still testing him. He tested him with failed crops, animals that died when giving birth, and failed vegetable gardens. He worked hard, but everyone else had an easier time. George could feel his frustration with every breath he took in the house. The adobe walls held the words of hurt and pain that his vati yelled at his mutti and his brothers.

As if his temper wasn't enough, he was able to hurt George and his brothers in a way incompatible with any vati-son relationship that they could have ever envisioned. The boys all knew that each of them suffered the same humiliation and abuse, but they didn't speak of it. It was shameful and made you look weak in the eyes of others. They just planned in their heads how to escape this act or seek revenge for it. On a sunny morning in June, George had returned late from picking up milk and delivering it to the cheese factory. He loved seeing other farmers, talking to others, and feeling like he was doing his part for the colony, even though he knew that being late would make his vati angry. There was fieldwork to do, but it didn't stop him from accepting pie from one of the other farmer's houses during his route, and it set his schedule back for the morning. Once he got back to his home farm, he ran with each step to get the horses tied up and get out to the field. He went into the barn to get the hoe and stumbled over his boots to walk faster, but it was too late. In the corner of the barn, he saw the shadow first, and then the eyes. His vati was waiting for him. They were alone.

He held the horse whip in one hand, and just as George registered the threat to his safety, he felt the snap of the whip across his lower legs, knocking him to the ground. A second snap came across his back as he laid on the ground with his hands over the back of his neck for protection. Johan walked closer, and George could hear his heavy breathing. He kicked him and told him to take off his overalls. George started to panic and yelled "no," and Johan whipped him again and again. He finally was too weak to resist, and his vati grabbed the straps of his overalls and pulled them down to reveal his bloody back and buttocks. He mounted him from behind and sodomized him. George could taste the dirt in his mouth as his face was being pushed into the soil on the barn floor. He felt a hot, rushing pain from the attack under the weight of his vati.

His vati's breathing and grunting were primal, and George could only take the assault and know that he would recover.

This wasn't the first assault, and knew this also happened to his brothers. When Jacob climaxed, he stopped. He pulled up his pants and kicked dirt onto George's back as he lay on the ground. His breathing was still rapid as George tried to pull up his overalls and stand. He could feel the pain on his back from the whip marks and in his rectum as he tried to stand. Johan waited for him to stand upright to meet his gaze. He had a darkness in his eyes that left no white. He was feeling powerful, and he grinned before walking away to the field. George picked up his hoe and followed him, limping and grimacing as he walked.

This was his vati's way of making sure he knew who was boss. He had been taught the same lessons by his vati. George never told anyone about this. It was a secret that would show shame and weakness to the elders. The men of the congregation and campos would have no interest in understanding the truth, only the words of the Bible. "Honour your mutti and vati" would be seen as the right answer, and so this sin would never be considered a flaw of Jacob's character, but instead a weakness in his sons for bearing the trauma publicly.

George's childhood. George Peter is second from the left in this photo with his brothers.

CHAPTER FIVE:
ANNA'S LIFE IN MEXICO

1953

Anna couldn't keep her legs straight for much longer. She was pushing her back against one wall and her feet against the other inside the old water well. It was about three feet across and one of the first wells that her vati had dug when they bought the property in 1924. It was dry now, like many of the wells in the campo. With her small but callused hand, she held onto a rope that was tied to the lid of the well and hung down about twenty feet. She was using it to help balance herself in case her legs got weak and she lost her grip. She had long legs for her five-foot-tall frame.

Anna leaned her head back against the dirt sides of the well to look up at the light threading through the wooden lid. It was a dark place, and only a little bit of light in long, thin threads was visible through the round well cover. The well had an odor of dampness and death and made Anna want to cough. The smell reminded her of the killing of chickens in the adobe shed when it was time to prepare them for eating. It was a fun, lively time of women boiling water to remove feathers and draining the blood from the decapitated birds while laughing and sharing stories. The moisture in the shed from the people and hot water brought out the smells in the soil, and today, it provided a specific smell that Anna was reminded of in this moment.

She wasn't alone in the well. Her sister Agatha was with her too. They were stacked almost on top of each other inside the well, alternating feet and

CHAPTER FIVE: ANNA'S LIFE IN MEXICO

back. They held onto the dangling rope, keeping their backs on the walls. They knew the rope was strong enough to pull them up and down because they had been in the well before. Their breath was starting to cause moisture to form in the already damp soil. Why would God ever make the soil red? Anna asked herself. Did He not know how hard it would be to clean it out of clothing? The smell of the soil was strong and tickled the back of Anna's throat, and she tried to stifle a cough. Even though it was dark in the well, she could see the whites of her sister's eyes looking at her to keep silent.

"Shhh" echoed in the well. Anna knew she needed to be quiet, but she hated that the Mexicans were here more often and that she had to hide. She knew why, but she hated it. She had to stay still and quiet until she heard the horses run off into the distance. It could anywhere from only a few more minutes or even hours, but she had to wait. Her mutti had prepared her and her sisters for their visits and taught them how to run to shelter when they heard the horses coming with the Mexicans. There were other times when they hid that they were found by the Mexicans, and it was never good for the girls, as they were often raped.

Anna was the second youngest girl in the family, but she had older brothers. They were with her vati, Johan, at the house as the women waited underground. She knew from experience that her brothers and her vati wouldn't be her protectors when the Mexicans arrived. They always brought alcoholic drinks called mezcal to get the Mennonites drunk. Anna shuffled and repositioned her legs on the dirt wall.

"Just a bit longer," Agatha said. "Sing your favourite hymn in your head, and when you're done, we can leave." Anna had to think over all the hymns from church and Sunday school that she knew. Once she started singing inside her head, her pitch felt off, too high, but in her mind, the backup singing was making it pretty darn perfect.

> *"Though the angry surges roll*
> *On my tempest-driven soul,*
> *I am peaceful for I know,*
> *Wildly though the winds may blow,*
> *I've an anchor safe and sure,*

That can evermore endure.

And it holds, my anchor holds:

Blow your wildest, then, O gale,

On my bark so small and frail;

By His grace I shall not fail,

For my anchor holds."

Anna started to laugh and quickly covered her mouth. She thought it was funny that she was singing about anchors holding as she hung onto a rope underground. She had heard of anchors in her Bible studies, but she couldn't even picture one. She had never seen the ocean or lakes and had certainly never been in a boat.

She was growing impatient. At the age of twelve, she had learned the lessons of when to speak and when to be quiet, but it really took everything in her to follow those rules.

Anna liked to be busy and productive. Not only was it in her bones, it was also expected of her as a Mennonite woman. She liked to be up early with her mutti to milk the cows and get the hens fed and gather eggs. Her older sisters were grown-up and married now, so she was the oldest girl with these jobs in the mornings and took the responsibility very seriously. Her mutti started with the baking and cleaning. She could have it. Anna was happiest talking to the animals. They enjoyed her company just as much. She was sure of it.

When she was underground, time went so slowly. She was able to hear a few words in Spanish as the Mexicans talked to her vati and brothers on the porch. She wasn't allowed to speak Spanish and would never dare speak anything but Plautdietsch, but she had picked up several words from overhearing her vati and brothers speak to the Mexicans.

The well was located about a hundred feet from the porch. The men knew it had dried up years before, and a cover had been put on it to keep children and animals from falling into it. Anna's mutti, Maria, had put a container of dirt on it a few years back and planted some flowers. She had planned it this way as a decoy for what lay beneath: a hiding spot for her daughters. Her vati, Johan, didn't understand that it was a hiding place, but he liked the flowers. He

CHAPTER FIVE: ANNA'S LIFE IN MEXICO

enjoyed the splash of colour in the barren yards of Chihuahua. The women in the colony all knew it was a safe place if they needed it, and there were several more throughout the campo.

Anna could hear one of the Mexicans ask, "*Donde estan las chicas?*" (Where are the girls?) She could hear feet walking above her head on the ground.

Anna's vati, Johan, was a man of few words. He grunted, "No concern of yours. Are you here to buy or to sell today?"

The Mexicans replied, "We've brought you a gift. We're just here for a visit today." They pulled out a full bottle of mezcal and opened the top. They smiled with their tobacco-stained teeth at Johan and his sons.

Johan was about the same height as the Mexicans and could look them right in the eye. He didn't like them at all and didn't try to hide it. But he knew that if he talked back to them, they might come back and take his livestock or burn his crops. He opened his mouth with a half smile and said, "We don't need to be drinking, but we'll enjoy your visit." His sons all nodded in agreement.

The Mexicans ignored him, and the first of the two men put the bottle to his dry lips and took a long sip ending with an "Ahh." He passed the bottle to the second Mexican and then to Johan, who held the bottle for a moment while looking at the smiling visitors. He took one small sip and smiled at the men, holding up the bottle to toast them. "*Tomar una bebida más grande*" (Take a bigger drink), they encouraged.

Their skin was dark from the summer sun, and they were unshaven. Johan was pale by their standards and wore a straw hat to keep the sun from burning his skin. He held the bottle in his hand tentatively and looked over to his sons. He knew that if he didn't participate in this game, his family could be robbed or beaten, and besides, he did like the taste of it. It burned as it went down, but it numbed him from his responsibilities and worries. In that moment, he thought to himself, *Where are Maria and the girls?* He didn't know. Women kept a lot of secrets among themselves. That thought made him tense up. They had no right to be keeping secrets from the men.

He lifted the bottle to his lips and took a long drink. It burned as it went down his throat but soothed him at the same time. He shook his head and passed the bottle to his sons. They all mirrored what their vati had done, each of them shaking their head with some coughing. When the bottle made it back to the Mexicans, it was half empty. They drank again, but only a half a mouthful and passed it on. They wanted the Mennonites to have most of it. The Mexicans knew that the Mennonites weren't supposed to be drinking and couldn't handle their alcohol very well. They took pleasure in watching their weakness show. They were hardworking men who took many acres of land from the Mexicans, but they could be taken to the ground with one bottle of mezcal.

The girls could hear faint talking and laughter from their hiding place underground. It was getting harder for Anna to keep her legs on the wall as time went on. Her sister Agatha was the closest to the top of the well, as it was the narrowest part and her legs were shorter. At fifteen, Agatha was the smallest and youngest. Anna had always been the baby in the family until her sister came along. It was a battle between them to see who the prettiest, smartest, and best baker and cleaner would be. Anna felt threatened by Agatha and hoped secretly that she would slip down the well a little bit to get more dirt on her.

Johan could feel the effects of the booze and summer sun on his head. He took a chair on the porch, and his sons sat on the ground. They were all feeling the effects of the mezcal and chatting in Spanish. The Mexicans stood tall over them as they sat and drank the last mouthful of alcohol. Jacob leaned his head back against the house with his brown hair blowing in the summer heat. He closed his eyes just for a little rest. His boys were already sleeping on the porch. Their denim overalls were all the same and lined up like clothes on a clothesline. They leaned on each other to rest as the summer afternoon heat reached its peak.

Anna and her parents adhered to a particular "Ordnung," a system of rules and expectations on how to live their lives. These rules were enforced by the pastor and elders and were laid out in the Bible. To stay in the campo, everyone had to follow the rules and attend meetings and church. Adhering to the Ordnung was a part of their daily rituals. Today, however, many rules were broken. It didn't take long before Jacob and his sons were sleeping, and the Mexicans started searching the house and yard for the girls. They would take any food that was prepared. Mennonite homes had minimal furniture, and they had no interest in taking heavy objects.

Mainly, they had come for the girls. Mennonite girls were forbidden to have any contact with Mexicans, and this made them irresistible. It was also a way for the Mexicans to show their dominance over these people. If they could have their women, they would be better men than the ones laid out on the

CHAPTER FIVE: ANNA'S LIFE IN MEXICO

porch. They looked in the bedrooms and shed and couldn't find them. They started to scheme about where they would be hiding as they stood next to the flowerpot in the yard. "*Estúpidos menonitas desperdiciando agua en una maceta de flores. No puedes comer flores.*" (Stupid Mennonites, wasting water on a pot of flowers. You can't eat flowers.)

The sweat was pouring down the girls' foreheads as they huddled beneath the Mexicans' feet in the well shaft. The white of the flowers on their dresses were turning a cayenne colour from the soil within the well. Mexico in July was a hot place, and the only benefit to being underground was that it was a bit cooler. Still, Anna didn't like being dirty. She tried to brush the soil from her dress and white ankle socks, but it only made the red smear to a pink tone, so she stopped. She would need to wash all this clothing when they got out of the well.

That day, when the Mexicans came, Anna's mutti had caught sight of the horses before she could hear them. The area was pretty barren between campos, and you could see visitors coming for miles because of the dust rising up with every step of the horses' hooves. No electricity lines spanned the landscape of dusty roadways, no cars were seen; only buggies and horses waving their tails in the pasture to keep the flies away. Her mutti knew that she had only a little time to get herself and her daughters out of the house to safety. In the past, before she understood what the Mexicans wanted, she'd let the girls stay. But never again. Word had spread between the women quickly on the dangers, and they had come up with a plan to warn each other if they were to see the Mexicans coming.

Sometimes, they weren't prepared. When the Mexicans could see that the men were no threat to them, asleep and drunk on mezcal, they'd attacked Maria, Johan's wife. She yelled for the girls to run, but there was confusion and scampering, ands all of them were caught. She was physically held back with hands on her chest as she watched the men touch her girls' hair and then hold up their pleated dresses to touch their white legs. She yelled for them to stop, but Jacob didn't wake up, so she started kicking. She used the Spanish that she had learned from overhearing her husband do business to direct them away from her children. "*Deja en paz a esos bebés y ven a buscarme. Se un hombre de verdad.*" (Leave those babies alone and come and get me. Be a real man.)

They turned and she looked at them, saying in Plautdietsch, "*Schwein noagel.*" Pig tail, slang for dirty, unkempt men. "Run, girls." The men were pleased that had Maria stopped fighting them, and they started to fondle her breasts, undoing the bobby pins in her hair. Her long, brown hair unfolded from the pins to waist-length braids. They lifted her skirt and apron to reveal her bare legs and to draw the attention to herself. She wasn't kicking anymore. She knew that if they were pleased with her, her daughters would get away. She would just pray in her head. Pray that God was watching and wouldn't give her more than she could endure. All the while, her husband and sons slept only a few feet from them.

When the Mexicans left and her husband awoke, he wouldn't believe the stories. He said that the women brought it on themselves, and that Maria was raising whores for daughters. Johan had been ashamed when he heard the story and couldn't even look at her. He shook his head in disbelief and left the house. He staggered to the barn with his head still swimming from the alcohol. He couldn't tell anyone about this. His family would never be accepted. He would keep this quiet, and he would pray that his wife would be forgiven.

Maria knew that she would do everything possible to keep this from ever happening again. She alone had to look after herself and her daughters. It wasn't the same Mexicans who came every time, but they all seemed to know how to find the weakness in the men on the campos and understood how to manipulate the submissiveness of the women to force them to do what they wanted. The women would only share their stories among the other women. If the elders found out they had sex with Mexicans, they would be shunned, and it would ruin their lives and their families.

In the campo, a young girl had been violated by the Mexicans and was too ashamed to tell her family. She became pregnant, and she and her mutti hid it from her vati and pastors. News in the Mennonite community of her pregnancy would mean shunning her and her never being able to secure a husband. This wasn't the first pregnancy of a young Mennonite girl that was unmarried. When she went into labour, she had another Mennonite midwife attend and delivered in the barn, far from the eyes of the men. Her baby was born healthy, with mahogany-coloured skin and dark eyes. She never held the baby. The elder Mennonite women and her mutti wrapped the baby, and then it was silently tucked into the carriage. The older women harnessed the horses and buggy, and with the snap of the whip, they took the baby away. They rode out into the desert and laid the baby on the red sandy soil on its own. They looked away as

CHAPTER FIVE: ANNA'S LIFE IN MEXICO

they drove home, ignoring the howl of the wolves that crept closer, drawn by the baby's cry.

The rape and birth would never be discussed, but the women knew. It was part of the world they discussed during their quiet times quilting or baking together. They could share their suffering then, knowing that if the men or church leaders knew, their lives would be forever changed. Secrets meant that they could keep the life that was sacred to them, their culture, and their future.

That day, when Maria had seen them coming, she cried out to "hide now" and rang the bell on the house. The bell was the signal for other women in nearby farms to take cover and for her girls to run behind the house to the old well. When the men heard the bell, they would only think that it was lunchtime. They knew it seemed early, but they came in from the fields. With only horse-and-plow equipment, the bell could be heard for miles in the fields. The girls dropped what they were doing and ran. They pushed the flower box aside, took the rope, and lowered themselves. Maria's heart was racing as she watched them and then looked over her shoulder at the Mexicans and the men to make sure no one saw the girls run. Even her husband didn't know of the hiding place.

As the girls pulled the lid over the well, Maria ran. It was the woman's work to look after the chickens, so she had built a hiding spot that only she knew about. She quickly crawled into her dugout beneath the bags of grain for chicken food. She had a barn board over the opening, and she slid it over and then tucked herself under it. She lay on her back with the smell of chicken feces on her and her hands, and she pulled the board weighted with grain over her. She knew she needed to lay still. If she heard the Mexicans coming near her girls, they would call out, and then she would save them by offering herself. She was already married and "used up," so she didn't care anymore, but her girls should be protected or they would never get a husband.

She breathed heavily and heard the Mexicans walking around the yard. Her husband must be drunk by now, she thought to herself. How could they be so dumb to do this over and over? Maria took a deep breath and nearly coughed with the smell of chicken feces. She could feel the pressure in the back of her head from her *dietscha ssoppen*, her braid, and the pins holding it in place. *Next time, take out bobby pins,* she told herself. Thoughts were racing through her head, and panic was starting to form in her gut. She could feel her heart racing. Was everyone okay, or had they found the girls?

NOT MY KIND OF MENNONITE

The Mexicans opened the chicken coop inside the shed and quickly looked around, talking in Spanish between themselves. "*Esos hombres no dormirán demasiado, date prisa.*" (Those men won't sleep too long, hurry up.) She held her breath as they walked near her hiding place. "*Tado claro.*" (Nothing here.) She could hear their boots on the dirt near her, and then they turned and walked out, leaving the door open. The chickens were running outside to forage for seeds. She could hear their feet scurrying and sifting the soil. She would stay a bit longer. The Mexicans didn't even know enough to shut the chicken coop doors behind them until the eggs were collected.

Anna was feeling hot and restless again, scratching her head. She could feel dirt falling into her hair from the sides of the well. When could they come out? It had been a game at first, but now, after waiting for half an hour, it was getting hard to stay put. Anna knew that she had to keep her back strong and her legs up. The muscles were starting to quiver in her thighs as they got weaker. But still, she and Agatha waited, hearing feet walking and then horses' hooves on the ground. The horses ran past, and then the sound became more distant.

Agatha lifted the well cover to the side very carefully before putting her head out enough to see. "Come now. Let's get to the house."

A wave of hot desert air hit Anna's face as she crawled to the surface. She wiped the red dust from her face and shook her braids to get the dirt out. The coast was clear, and they started walking toward the house, looking left and right to make sure they wouldn't be surprised by Mexicans who might have been hiding. At the house, Anna saw her vati sleeping in a chair. His head was leaning back against the house, and he was snoring. Her brothers were lying on the porch floor, also sleeping and breathing deeply. The hammock gently swung back and forth with the hot winds above their heads.

As the girls went into the house, they could hear scurrying footsteps from across the yard. Mutti was running to them from the chicken coop as she dusted the dirt from her hair and dress. "Get in the house and shut the door, girls," she yelled breathlessly. She panicked as she saw them and frantically turned her head from side to side to make sure no one was hiding in the yard to surprise them later. Maria quickly checked their dresses and hair when they got into the house. "No one got to you, did they?" The girl shook their heads no. All was good. The women smiled to each other in a knowing way and nodded. They

CHAPTER FIVE: ANNA'S LIFE IN MEXICO

weren't always safe, and they knew this wouldn't be the last time they would have to hide.

Maria was quick to take charge of the house and started the girls with the tasks of cleaning up and getting the bread ready for dinner. She brushed the dirt from her midcalf-length pleated dress. It would come clean in the wash. Dark colours like purple made the dirt less obvious. She put on her black head kerchief and washed her hands in the water pail at the side of the sink. She was smiling as she worked to get the flour out for tortillas and buns because she was pleased that she had outsmarted the Mexicans again and that no one got to her or the girls. God was good to them that day.

As the girls prepared for the meal by setting the table and wiping down the oil cloth, the men lay outside. Anna's vati was a hardworking man who tried very hard to avoid temptation, follow the word of God, and raise his family. But, like everyone else, he had his weaknesses.

CHAPTER SIX:
MARRIAGE PREPARATIONS

1959

George and Anna had been trying to be more public to avoid rumours and pressure from families to marry, so after church, they would talk. George had asked Gerhard, Anna's brother, about Anna and was trying to understand her personality and what life with her would be like. Anna's vati had been speaking with George's vati about the rumours that George and Anna were alone together and engaging in inappropriate activities. The elders felt it was best if they married to reduce controversy, ensuring both families saved face in the eyes of the colony.

Now when they spoke, there was pressure on George to move forward with his intentions, and Anna couldn't have been more delighted. She really wanted to be his wife. In her family, she was always seen as the one who was slower at everything, and even though she was more flirtatious than was acceptable in the traditions of the congregation, she was pretty determined that George was going to be her husband and that her life would be better than other girls in her campo. She had visions of the perfect home, clean and with bread always in the oven, with many children running around. She would be respected by her parents, sisters, and other women for her skills and place in the community. She could daydream about this for hours.

Usually, courtships were short. Long courtships were unfavourable in the eyes of the pastors. Everyone knew each other, and families were already familiar,

CHAPTER SIX: MARRIAGE PREPARATIONS

so there was no need to take time to form relationships with families before marrying. The expectation was that each set of parents would provide added support and teaching, which would ensure that the couple understood their commitment to each other, their families, their community, and the church. The pastor would then give his blessing to go forward with the marriage.

George and Anna would have a good standing in the colony if a marriage was proposed and a wedding occurred in a quick and appropriate manner. This quick wedding would change the conversation in the community away from the rumours, allowing the families to maintain their status and giving George and Anna a supported union.

Anna was frustrated because as much as she wanted to look her best and act her best, George hadn't said a word to her since she had asked him to take her kerchief. Even though there was pressure for their marriage, she wanted to keep this part of the traditions and show off her embroidery skills. She was afraid that he might be talking to her brother when they did chores together and change his mind about marrying her. She knew they judged her based on how smart she was. She was pretty perfect, though. The voices in her head confirmed this daily. Only chosen people had special voices right from God. She knew she was special, and she wanted to keep the voices to herself. It was like having a friend or consciousness talking in one ear all the time. The voices also told her they would hurt her if she told others what they talked about. The voice was always a male, so it had to be God. He spoke softly most of the time. She wouldn't share this with anyone. It would protect the relationship between God and herself if she was quiet about it.

Anna's and George's families were to meet after church on a Sunday to plan the wedding. One week before the wedding, the bride's and groom's parents met. The men discussed homes, farms, and work, and the women talked about how the bride would fit in with the household, the wedding meal, and her dress. The couple would traditionally stay with the grooms' parents until they had enough money of their own for a home. If they were able to work all of this out, George and Anna would be married the following week. During the week, the bride or groom could change their mind or find another woman or man if they felt it wasn't a good match.

Anna was eighteen years old and had a very small circle of friends. Because she was pretty and took good care of her clothing, men looked at her, and she knew that she could be a good wife. Other women weren't as friendly to her because of her impulsive actions and her temper. She liked to have things a certain way, and if someone sat in the wrong spot during church, she couldn't seem to get over it. She would ask herself why everyone tested her like that. Why was God testing her like that? Anyone else might have shrugged it off, but she couldn't. She had to correct it. This was why she had so few friends. Her parents would put a hand to her shoulder and hold her in the pew in church to keep her from walking over to make someone move.

Her mutti had more patience and so she tried to manage Anna. Her vati was shorter tempered with her. He had two full years of failed crops behind him and had to start working for local Mexicans in the watermelon fields to earn enough to keep his home and pay the colony. He had also started drinking alcohol in the fields to help numb the pain of his failure. He kept a bottle on him, and the Mexicans always had some available. He would pay half his daily wages for this, but he also knew that the drink was worth it to keep him walking tall and proud in his community and cover up his anxiety and fear about what the future would hold for his family.

Anna had grown up doing her share of the chores. With only two girls at home now, she had to help out more to get the work done. Her vati was often sleeping outdoors after his work, and her mutti was laid in bed sleeping or having her legs up with her bulging veins and weeping skin from the added pressure from standing all day. She knew from watching her own mutti how to treat this type of condition. She would wrap her legs tightly in white fabric to look like stockings and wash them daily.

Sometimes, when Anna was outside, helping feed the chickens, her older brother Heinrich cornered her in the barns alone. He held her down and pulled up her dress and apron to expose her. She tried to push him away, but he held his hand over her mouth, not letting her speak. He told her that it was her job to do as a man says. He then raped her, being careful not to put his seed inside her, and then tossed her aside. "*You ne Hua.*" (Whore.) "You will never have a good man the way you act."

She looked at him as he zippered up his pants. She knew that he could take what he wanted, and her vati would beat her for accusing him of the act. She hoped that when she was married, it would stop. Heinrich knew that no one

CHAPTER SIX: MARRIAGE PREPARATIONS

would listen to her because of the stories she told from her head, so no one would believe his assault on her.

Getting married would help her find her own way of keeping a house and being a wife instead of always having to subject herself to these assaults as part of her role as a woman. She knew that raising this to others including her mother, would only lead to her being held back from being prepared as a wife for men in the colony. She could leave the forced sexual advances from men in the colony behind and just please her husband. Her wedding day would be all about her and her devotion to God and George, just as her sisters before her. She was excited to have the attention, even though it wasn't something the pastor would approve of. Maria and Anna were both hoping for a successful wedding, each of them with their own dreams of a life different from the one they were leading.

This Sunday morning was a bit hectic in preparing food for the meal with the Peters family. It was acceptable to be social on Sundays; many families would visit neighbours, and the children would get to play and enjoy the day without chores. Of course, the farm animals had to be fed every day, but hoeing in the fields or hauling milk to the cheese factory could wait for this day to be over.

Agatha watched Anna get dressed. Anna was very quiet, which meant that she was nervous or planning something. Agatha knew this from her life with her sister. Anna was very proud of her clothes, keeping everything well-pressed. Anna had watched her mutti and her grandmutti prepare patterns and fabric for new dresses and mend older clothing. This tradition was important to the women in her family as a way of ensuring other traditions were maintained and kept in their secluded community in the shadow of the mountains.

Anna enjoyed sewing and pressing clothes. She liked the precision involved with a good stitch and straight hem or line. It pleased her to see perfection in her dresses and how she sewed them. She would redo seams many times to get the perfect look and be satisfied it was done correctly. Anna's mutti grew tired of the repetitious stitching, and the fabric was threadbare in some areas from ripping out stitches as she sought perfection. But Anna couldn't imagine why she would wear something that wasn't perfect in every way. Everyone would look. She had many brothers and knew that they acted differently from her. She knew that they could do more because they were men, and she envied their freedom.

Freshly washed faces and clean white scarves were the images of Christian purity that the Mennonites were proud of. In Mexico, it wasn't as hard for the Mennonites to be seen as different from the native inhabitants of the area, and it was important to maintain this distinction. The traditional clothing of the Mexican women was too fashionable for the Mennonite women and would have been linked to Satan as sexual temptation and individual identity.

Agatha was trying on one dress, then another, but the buttons wouldn't fasten because her breasts were developing, and the dresses were too small. She couldn't have any skin showing between the hem of her dress and the tops of her white socks. This would draw unwanted attention to her developing body and white skin. There was always the risk of losing the church membership for herself and her family if she wore clothing that didn't meet the guidelines of conformity and obedience. Agatha kept trying on dresses, one after the other. She wasn't as particular about her dress being too tight when working around the house and barns, but at church, there was added pressure to conform.

Anna watched Agatha from across the room, smiling in approval at her sister's struggles. She had spent so much time making sure her dresses were lovely and better than anyone else's, and now she could watch Agatha's problems with personal pride. Agatha always had an easier life than Anna—at least, so she thought. She got along well with other girls, and her sisters had her over to help look after children, and so did other young muttis. Agatha smiled a lot and took pleasure in fitting in with others, which had never come easy to Anna.

Agatha continued to try on one dress after another, threw them onto the bed, and continued to search for another dress. Agatha was expected to do more chores around the house, read the Bible, and keep up with studies as she could for school. Anna didn't have the same expectations because she couldn't learn as quickly, but she was assigned time to perfect her mending and embroidery.

"You have many dresses that no longer fit you, Anna. Could you share them with me?" asked Agatha.

Anna turned her head quickly to look at her sister. "No. These are my dresses, and you can't have any of them. You have to make your own dresses." *Let's see who the better wife will be, after all.*

"But you can't even wear them anymore. You could share them," stammered Agatha.

CHAPTER SIX: MARRIAGE PREPARATIONS

Anna walked to her dresser and looked at the dresses she no longer wore. She took them out and laid them across the bed. She had great skill with a thread and needle, and they all had perfect pleats and hems. She looked at them and back at her sister several times. She then left the room without saying anything, walked to the kitchen, and got the scissors from the drawer. Back in their room, she laid the dresses one at a time on the wooden floor. Her sister watched intently as she put them down and then picked up the scissors and started cutting them from the bottom to top.

Agatha lunged forward. "Stop it. Don't wreck them!" she yelled.

Anna kept cutting. She used her elbow to push Agatha off of her, and soon, the dresses were just shredded strips of fabric. As she was cutting, she smiled. Agatha might have been younger than her and smarter as well, but she wouldn't have her dresses and get compliments on Anna's hard work.

Anna's mutti heard the yelling and came into the room. She stood tall in the doorway and looked at the girls on the floor. "What's going on? What have you done, Anna?" she asked as she kneeled on the floor. She put her hand out to take the scissors from her daughter, who pulled them away from her. She reached again and grabbed the scissors this time, pulling them from Anna's grip.

Agatha started to cry. "I asked her if I could have her old dresses, and she just started cutting them up. The devil is in her."

Anna was on her knees, her eyes on the ground. It was different when her mutti was unhappy with her. She said nothing.

"Anna, why did you do this?" her mutti asked. "This is good, expensive fabric, and your sister needs dresses. We can't be wasting money like this. We don't have enough for more dresses." She came closer to Anna on the floor. She picked up the fabric pieces and grew angrier as she picked up the dresses that were now cut apart. She slapped Anna across the face. Anna didn't flinch. "You will pick this up and you will sew it back together tomorrow, not on the Lord's Day. You will mend this dress and wear it." Anna stood up and looked down on her mutti while holding her cheek. Her mutti grabbed the fabric in her arms and threw it at Anna. "Put this in your sewing basket and get yourself dressed for church."

Agatha and their mutti went through the remaining dresses and found three more for Agatha. "These will be nice on you," her mutti said. Agatha wiped the tears from her freckled cheek and gave a small smile. "Your sister can be very jealous. The devil makes her do things. Pray for her. Let's get you dressed for church."

Anna knew what was expected of her, but it was really hard. She often had thoughts in her head about what to say and what to do, but they weren't always what she was supposed to do. She liked to be liked and to fit in, but that had never really happened. She didn't understand just sitting in silence, embroidering or sewing, when you could tell or share stories. Her mutti hushed her often, but she couldn't do it.

Not only did she have a lot of thoughts, but she also had a lot of words spoken just for her. She listened intently and began to hear another person in her head around the same time as she was planning her marriage and life with George. She heard angel voices and devil voices. She knew which was which based on the response of people around her. It was hard to know what to listen to, but she felt that God had chosen her to be special, and she needed to make sure she followed His plan for her. He wouldn't allow any harm to come to her or her life with these extra voices. She knew that He wanted her to go to heaven, so she took the time to listen and follow the voices when she wasn't sure which direction to go. She had faith that God would show her the way.

Anna didn't like helping her sister in any way. Why should she? She was chosen to be special by God. She had voices in her head now that told her how special she was and how others, like Agatha, weren't to be trusted or loved. Her inner voice had told her many times that Agatha was out to destroy her life.

Her voices were only for her. This meant she was special. No one else could hear the voices, and therefore, they didn't know she was chosen to represent God on earth.

Anna put on her best dress with her back to Agatha and watched her mutti walk out. She put a white handkerchief around her hair for church. When Anna's parents moved to Mexico, they were still wearing bonnets, but with the weather, wind conditions, and heat, the congregation decided it was favourable to wear a scarf in place of the bonnet. On more informal outings, they could wear a wide-brimmed straw hat. According to the Bible, Corinthians 11, women had to have their heads covered during worship in recognition of their subordinate place in the universe. After baptism and marriage, the scarf colour changed to signify their baptism and devotion to God and a deeper understanding of their duties to man and God.

CHAPTER SIX: MARRIAGE PREPARATIONS

Anna was putting the final touches on her dress and hair—two bobby pins in her hair, mostly to hold it from her face, but also because it looked fancier. She took pride in her hair, and so did her vati. He believed women shouldn't cut their hair, and he often had a say in how his daughters' hair was styled. Anna wiped the dust from her dress that had surfaced with the gust of wind through the glassless window and left the room without looking back at her sister, who was putting on the best dress from Anna's collection.

Anna walked into the kitchen to find her mutti frantically wrapping the baking in tea cloths. Maria was still angry about the fighting between her daughters. Anna could tell by the way she was breathing and roughly tossing the bread into the basket. She had been cooking all Saturday to prepare for the faspa with the Peters family. Maria didn't have much hope that the wedding would go forward because of the way her daughter acted. She could have Anna at home forever, she thought to herself as she tied the cloth around the basket of food and repinned her hair.

Anna wouldn't be a good mutti or wife. She had an anger in her eyes that made them go dark. She knew Anna heard voices because she had seen her talking to herself and smiling when she worked in the garden. It wasn't a natural smile. Maria had seen it in her own family members years before. There wasn't enough prayer to help this go away. God would turn on her eventually; there was only so much patience in any human or spirit for this type of personality. God had ways to making sure you paid your dues in life. Maria had felt it herself. She suffered with despair often in her life, and now, as she was finally getting her children married and having time to herself, her daughter was afflicted with voices that might never leave her.

Anna was daydreaming as she walked out to the buggy for church and had to go back to the kitchen and get the food baskets that Maria had laid out. She was hoping that her vati would like George's vati. They had known of each other for years, working together building barns and selling cattle. They were both hardworking men.

Anna's vati was sitting in the buggy, waiting for the women and quietly drinking from the glass bottle tucked inside his overalls, before they finally arrived. What was taking so long? He didn't know about the dress cutting, the fights, or the food preparation. He only knew that he had already milked the cows, fed them, cleaned the buggy, and brushed the horses. It was important to have a clean buggy and well-groomed horses for church. People would notice and talk if the animals were too thin or someone drove a dirty wagon. Anna's vati was very proud, and it was important that he be regarded as a good member of the community.

Anna was worried about her hair and dress as they sat in the buggy. She tried not to look at Agatha. She was angry with her for getting their mutti involved in the disagreement. She wanted their mutti to think she was better than Agatha. It was a sin to hold herself in higher regard than another, but Anna couldn't help it. The feelings, the anger, had all came quicker and more frequently in the last year.

The horses knew the way, but the wind was blowing red dirt in their faces and in the air. Anna worried that she wouldn't look her best when she arrived and tried to hold her scarf around her neck and her dress down to her knees.

They went into the church and had their service. Anna knew that the German sermon was meant for her. She could feel the presence of other beings from God near her during the service. She could hear her voices in her head saying "Amen." She knew that even though others might not know it, she was destined for a more blessed life than anyone there. She would be the one everyone talked about at church and in the community.

After church, they loaded again into the buggy and started their journey to the Peters home. When they arrived, Jacob, George's vati, was outside on the porch. He walked toward them and nodded his head. George came running out of the house to see them. He didn't want to seem too excited, but he had grown accustomed to the idea of marrying Anna and knew that Gerhard, her brother, was a good man. Therefore, Anna would be a good wife. He had only spoken a few sentences to her before he accepted her kerchief, but he wasn't a man of many words to begin with, and it seemed like enough. She wasn't a bad-looking woman, and her mutti kept a good house and would have taught Anna how to cook and clean. That was the most important thing in his mind as he saw her family get out of their buggy.

Gerhard had warned him about her moods and that he might have to manage her behaviour to keep her within the rule of the church. George wasn't worried, as he felt his work outside and hers wouldn't lead to him having to deal with her moods. He had lots of work he could do outdoors to earn extra money and see his friends.

CHAPTER SIX: MARRIAGE PREPARATIONS

George walked toward the buggy and helped Anna's mutti, Agatha, and then Anna to the ground. Their eyes met, and they exchanged a small smile. Then, he looked away. They all walked in, with Anna's vati being the last so he could talk with Jacob. They were talking about crops and land when they entered the house. The girls quickly went to the kitchen to help George's mutti, Gertruda.

She smiled and welcomed them, and then they placed their baking and bread on the table. "Thank you for what you have brought."

Each of them knew their role and set the table and prepared pickles and relishes to go with the meat. Anna was trying hard to make a good impression so that her potential new mutti-in-law would like her. Agatha was also trying to be tidy and efficient so that when it was her turn, she could marry Johan, George's brother. Anna sensed the competition and had to hold in her anger toward her sister. This wasn't her day. She wasn't going to win Gertruda over before Anna had a chance. She elbowed Agatha away from setting the table. Her sister moaned from the sharp poke of Anna's elbow to her ribs. Anna's mutti watched them and gave them a look of fierceness. Anna couldn't wreck this. She would never find another man to have her.

 Living in one Mennonite home was pretty much the same as living in another. They kept the houses clean, shared the same recipes, and knew the value of being quiet so the men could talk during and after dinner. Anna arranged the meat on a platter while Gertruda watched her. *She would do*, Gertuda thought to herself. She could bear many children, and she knew that God was important in her life. It was hard to think of her son being married because it would soon mean that all four of her sons would be finding a partner. She loved her role in managing the home and would teach Anna the same way so her son would be happy. She had no daughters, so this would be an adjustment for her.

Gertruda had also heard stories about Anna and knew that her tempers and words got her into trouble in the church. George would have to train her in how to be a good wife and keep quiet when she wasn't asked to speak. It could be done. She was trainable, and Gertruda knew that if George learned from his vati, a fist or slap would soon get her in line with what the community expected. Living in the same house with Jacob would soon show Anna how to act, and she would be welcome to take some of the blows that had been given to Gertruda over her years of marriage.

As the table was prepared for faspa, Anna was anxious to find a seat close to George. She did her best to sit close to him, but the men sat at one side of the table and women sat on the other. She ate her dinner as politely as she could and tried to not say anything unless her parents told her to. After dinner, the families continued to talk about farms, where a good farm would be for Anna and George in the future, and how they would help with the main farm as well. When dinner and talking was done, the men nodded at each other and then toward George. This was the approval that they were looking for. The wedding could proceed.

After this acknowledgement, they got back into the horse and buggy and headed back to church for the evening service. Anna sat up tall in her pew and George in his, both of them facing forward with separate dreams of what their lives would become.

CHAPTER SEVEN:
WEDDING AND PREPARATIONS

1959

George couldn't be late that day. As he entered the barn, Gerhard was already there.

"Hey, lazy," yelled his best friend and soon-to-be brother-in-law. They had been friends since childhood and saw each other at church weekly. They were now grown men, and although Gerhard was married to Margaret and expecting his first child, he and George still spent much time together while working. As men, they worked, played, hunted, and told stories. George knew that no matter what, Gerhard would have his back, and he would have Gerhard's. Life could be hard in the colonies, but friendships were what bound the men together. It made them strong and helped them find ways to make ends meet when the weather or crops weren't behaving.

Gerhard walked alongside George, who stood at least three inches taller. They started with the milking, each grabbing a stool. It wasn't a bad job in the mornings. The cows were happy to see them, their teats full of milk. Life in Cuauhtémoc was a struggle for the Mennonites, and they felt as though they would forever be *fremden*, or foreigners, even though Mexican officials didn't mind them settling into the country. His family only wanted peace, and they

CHAPTER SEVEN: WEDDING AND PREPARATIONS

had to be on guard to stay within the religious practices and not be tempted by Mexican ways.

George sat, milked, and talked with Gerhard. "Our parents have permitted a wedding between Anna and me." He made this statement and watched Gerhard's face for a reaction. He got nothing from him and kept rhythmically milking the cow. He then asked, "Do you think Anna is a good wife for me?"

Gerhard continued milking without looking up. "She was raised at home to cook and clean, but she's had problems fitting in and knowing what a woman is supposed to do in the home and community. Our mutti has taught her how to look after the gardens and farm animals."

George and Gerhard let the cows out of the barn to the colony pasture when they were done milking. As he carried out this ritual, George reflected on how marriage might help his life. He wasn't sure if he loved Anna, but he didn't really know what love had to do with marriage and having children. He didn't see many couples together that he would say "loved" each other. Marriage was a duty. Anna was willing to marry him, and he was desperate for a life of his own.

Gerhard continued to talk about Anna. "Mutti makes sure she follows the Bible and tries to help her with her Bible reading and work. She's not too smart with books, but she can make good bread."

George nodded and raised his eyebrows. Was that as good as it got? At least he could move out of the family home if he was married. He was able to find an adobe shed that would be suitable as a first house after he was married. He could have his own life and get away from his vati. He needed to get out of there because as his vati's drank more, his attacks on George increased. He didn't know how his mutti put up with all of it, but she did. She was a woman of God, but she couldn't protect her boys or herself. She could only pray more.

George knew what to expect from a wife, as it was laid out in the colony by the elders. Women should know when to speak and what to do in the eyes of the community to be considered a good Christian and wife. He knew that the elders taught them that any wife could have a voice in the home, but only when called upon. She shouldn't be free to give her opinions unless her vati or husband asked for them. He was ready to start fresh. He hoped for a better life with Anna. Maybe in being a bit slow, she would just do as she was told and not question him, he silently thought.

He also didn't want to bring Anna to his home to live there, and he tried to find another place for them to live. Traditionally, all men of a family would be given their own land to start farming, but with drought and poor success, there was no land for George to have at this time. Many homes sat empty, fields without crops, as other families were migrating back to Canada and some farther south to Paraguay. The wells were drying up, and with their congregation still believing in their old ways, many couldn't succeed. Some were excommunicated as they joined other more progressive colonies.

George and Anna had made their intention of marriage known to the pastor at the church. In just a two-week period, the wedding was organized, and the pastor was having regular teachings with George and Anna about the vows and duties of marriage. The responsibilities to each other were God-given, and the husband would always be considered the head of the home. The woman was responsible for birthing many children and submitting to their husbands for sex as he required. The pastor repeated to them each session that the main source of unhappiness in the home lay in the woman's unwillingness to submit to her husband as God had commanded. George and Anna sat quietly, listening and nodding in agreement. This was essential for the pastor to move ahead with the wedding ceremony. If they had sex before the wedding and baptism, they would have to confess to the pastor and promise not to do it again until they were officially married. Anna would only be allowed to wear a white kerchief if she was a virgin, and she would keep this on until after the baptism and the wedding. The pastor had also heard the rumours about George and Anna, so he wanted them to reflect on the kerchief colour to ensure there was honesty and integrity in the service and how they were accepted into the colony.

Anna had started adding items to her trousseau, which included her embroidered tea towels. Her sisters also prepared items for her new home such as pottery cooking pots. The best of the gifts was a quilt that her mutti gave her. Her mutti had been working on wedding quilts for all of her girls. She had her neighbours and friends help with the top stitching so she could display their individual styles and crafts. This quilt was the prized one in Anna's collection. She had a few smaller ones she had made herself for her first home, but they were made mostly of dark fabrics she had been able to buy and borrow from others. It reflected her moods and would be warm but certainly not as admired.

CHAPTER SEVEN: WEDDING AND PREPARATIONS

On the day of their wedding, they had to sit in the *brutlied schotow*, a room for visitors before a wedding. Because they were newly baptized, they couldn't drink like some of the others were. In the eyes of the church, drinking and sinning should be left in the past when you got married.

After church, there was a dessert, and then they had faspa. It included favourites such as *tweebak* buns, *kringelkes* (twisted buns), *butta* (butter), jam and sugar cubes, *Schmaunt Küaken* (cookies), and instant coffee. All the bride's friends would bake for the *brutlied*, bride and groom, and they would eat with them. Anna didn't have many friends, so her sisters and mutti did most of the baking instead. A wedding cake wasn't be permitted as it was too fancy. All the unmarried girls set the tables, baked, chopped cabbage, and prepared head cheese the Friday before the wedding. The wedding was always on a Saturday. After faspa, people went home, and then around seven, the youth came back and have *komstborscht* (cabbage soup) for dinner with the *brutlied*.

Anna's family started preparations as soon as the families and pastor approved the marriage. They would touch up the paint on the doors, rake the yard. They would paint the bottom ten inches of the trees white around the front of the property. Faspa would be held at Anna's house for their family only. Anna, her mutti, and her sisters had prepared a brown dress with black edging for the wedding, conservative and proper for such an occasion. Her white kerchief was pressed and ready for her hair.

When the day was over, Anna and George were still not yet officially married. Anna would still sleep at her parents' house for the week until the Sunday after the wedding. During this week, Anna and George visited all their families and friends. They would have a full week to decide if they really wanted to be with each other. Anna was afraid that during this week together, George might find fault with her. She did her best to follow the rules, ignore the voices, and smile when she should be smiling. After the wedding and in the first week, they took the trip to Cuauhtémoc to get their marriage certificate and make their wedding legal.

On Sunday, a week after the wedding, Anna and George went to church. After church, they had their marriage confirmed. George had given Anna a kitchen table for a wedding gift. He would continue to work at the farm; they had been given a small building out back to rent. Anna proudly wore a black kerchief now since she was married.

Their life together was now beginning. In raising their own children, they both had hopes for a different life than what their parents were able to give them. Anna would learn quickly that she shouldn't expect too much from George. She could learn to love him, be submissive to him, and make a happy home. She would struggle with not sharing every thought and feeling in her head or what the voices were saying to her, but that was what the woman's circles and groups were for. Men didn't want to know what happened in a woman's mind. They didn't want to hear of the horror of childbirth and trivial matters.

Most importantly, George didn't want to know that the voices in Anna's head were getting louder.

Wedding Day photo, Mexico

CHAPTER EIGHT:
MARRIED LIFE IN MEXICO

1960

Anna knew that to keep a happy home, she needed faith in God, cleanliness, and to be an obedient wife in the eyes of the colony. She was okay with the first two. As for the last point, Anna had been trying her best, but the voices in her head were telling her she wasn't doing it right. She knew the voices were there to guide her and make sure she followed the word of God. Sometimes, she didn't agree with the voices, and she was afraid of what they would do to her if she didn't follow their directions. If the quiet voices were directly from God, then that meant that the loud, angry voices were from the devil. Anna tried hard to pay more attention to the voices from God, but sometimes, the other voices would be so loud and angry that the only way for her to keep them quiet was to follow their directions.

She had been listening to them tell her that her sewing wasn't good enough, that her bread didn't rise enough. The voices would usually only be there in the day, but now, she heard them all night too. They kept her up at night, and she had to go outside and listen to them to not wake up George. When she was home alone in the day, she would talk out loud to the voices. "I know that I can do better, and I will try. I don't want to be an awful wife."

You will always be an awful wife. Nothing you can do will make him happy. He will not lay in bed with you the way that you look now. He loves someone else.

CHAPTER EIGHT: MARRIED LIFE IN MEXICO

Anna was shocked when she heard this judgement from her voices. How could he possibly love someone else? They had only been married a few weeks. The voices were insistent that he was running around behind her back. This challenging talk from the voices was making her angry, and she needed clarity. She didn't have anyone to talk to now that they had moved into a house in a different campo several miles from her mutti.

Anna made up her mind about the information she'd received. She would just come out and ask George about his affairs. "He'll tell me if he doesn't love me and instead loves someone else," she reassured the voice. Anna had been sitting up at the kitchen table listening and thinking, and it was now 3 a.m. She was determined to silence the voices and settle this matter immediately. She had been tidying in the kitchen before she walked into the bedroom, and she could feel her anger rising inside her.

George was startled awake by the sound of Anna's breathing and her presence, standing over him. "What are you doing? It's the middle of the night. Come to bed," George said.

"Are you running around behind my back? I've heard that you are, and I need to know the truth," Anna stated, standing with her hands on her hips.

"Who have you been talking with? No. I'm working and trying to get us a good farm and crop. Shut up and go to bed."

Anna was happy with this response. She got into her nightgown and crawled in bed next to George. *I told you so*, she said inside her head. She pulled her nightgown around her feet by pulling her legs to her chest. She shivered from the night air and the cool cotton sheets.

When she was quiet and starting to get warm again from being outside, the voices came back.

You're gullible and will believe anything he says. You loser.

Anna opened her eyes and looked into the darkness. Why would the voices, who had always guided her to making the right choices, tell her this now? *I'll have to do better.* Anna closed her eyes and, realizing how exhausted she was, immediately went to sleep.

George lay in the darkness, hearing Anna's breathing slow down as she fell asleep. He wondered where she had heard the rumours. The colonies were full of rumours, but he knew Anna didn't have many friends. He thought of her standing over him at night with only the whites of her eyes visible and how it had suddenly scared him. With exhaustion creeping into the air, he let it go and joined her in sleep.

In the morning, Anna was too exhausted to get up to make George's breakfast. She had been up more hours at night with her thoughts, ruminating about her role as a wife. She could hear him in the kitchen, and he called her name.

"Anna, get up. I need my lunch made for the day and chores need to be done. Anna!"

She lay in bed and pretended not to hear. She was so tired.

Don't get up and don't do anything today. Stay in bed all day and don't listen to him. He's not your boss.

Anna agreed. She had nothing to prove and no energy to fight it. She lay in bed and pretended not to hear. She heard the door slam and George leave. At last, she was alone.

George ran to the horses to get the buggy hitched up. He didn't know what he was doing wrong. Being married was harder than he'd thought. He knew what was expected of a wife, and his friends all had wives who were able to keep the house and have dinner ready. Maybe he wasn't being strict enough. George met with his friends at the stable and talked to his brother-in-law, Gerhard.

"Anna wouldn't get up this morning to make my lunch or breakfast, and she was up in the middle of the night, yelling at me that I was fooling around behind her back. I don't know why she would think that. It's not really working out."

Gerhard looked at George as he grabbed his milking stool. "You have to set the rules early. Maybe she was spoiled at home. You need to let her know what you expect now. Keep her in line so you can do your work. You can't be up in the night and work all day with her still in bed. That's not right. She has work too."

George thought about his friend's advice. "You're right. I let her get away with sleeping in and not having my supper ready. This is happening more often lately. I need to be stricter and teach her how to be a wife." He pitched fresh hay into the mangers for the cattle and continued to work.

Later that evening, Anna was still lying in bed when she heard the front door open. Was George back? Who was there? Anna hid underneath the covers and then felt them being pulled off.

"Get out of this bed," yelled George.

Anna was confused. "What time is it? What's going on?" Her mind was racing, and she felt her heart race with anger. "Get out of here, you cheater. I

CHAPTER EIGHT: MARRIED LIFE IN MEXICO

don't have to do anything you say." She was on her knees on the bed and could hear the voices in her head telling her to protect herself and get away from him. She grabbed an oil lamp and started swinging it.

Hit him before he hits you.

He grabbed her arm, and she drew the other hand up and scratched his face, yelling, "Get off me! Get away!"

George was startled and, with an open hand, slapped her across the face with more force than he had intended. He drew his hand back again and looked in Anna's eyes. They were black and dark, and she had a smile on her face. He drew back, and she lifted the lamp and hit him on the side of his head. Blood was running down his temple, and he put his hand up to his forehead to hold the bleeding gash. Anna jumped up from under him and laughed.

Let's see who the tough guy is now. You're in charge now.

She took a deep breath and looked at her husband on the bed. She should run. And so, she did.

George didn't chase her. He was still in shock. How could his wife strike him? What was he doing wrong? This was shameful. He wouldn't be able to ask advice from his friends. He could never tell them that his wife hit him. That wasn't right for a man in this colony. He hung his head and heaved a big sigh. What would God want? How would He want George to manage this? He had no answers, but the elders would know. He cleaned up and left the home. He didn't care where Anna was. She could do what she needed to, but this wouldn't happen again.

Anna was still running when the voices yelled:

STOP! What are you doing? You're in charge here. Others know you're right. There's no need to run.

Anna stopped. Yes, that was right. She was in charge. She remembered the surprise on George's face when she'd struck him. It made her feel sad that she had treated her husband like that, but what choice did she have? She was listening to her conscience, and it was supposed to bring her closer to God.

She decided to walk to her mutti's house. She would understand and be able to help her with this. Her mother didn't understand her voices, but she could help her sort out what to do next. She knocked on the door and entered. It was growing dusk outside, and Anna's parents were sitting down for their main meal when she walked in.

Anna's mutti, Maria, looked up, surprised. "Hello. Welcome. What are you doing here this time of night?"

Anna's vati, Johan, had his back to her and turned his head around. "Where's George? Is he coming in with you?"

"No. I'm here alone. We had a fight." As she walked into the kitchen and the light shone on her face, her mutti and vati could see a bruise forming around her eye and the blood smeared across her forehead.

Johan stood up and looked at her. "What have you done now? Why is there blood on your face?"

Maria also stood and looked more closely at her daughter. "Anna, what is going on? Where's George?"

Anna started to sob. "I didn't like the way he treated me. He barged in and ripped the covers off me, and the voices said that I should hit him, so I did."

Her parents both looked at her in disbelief. "You hit your husband?" they said. "Why were you in bed? Did you have his dinner ready? You never hit a man." Johan was flushed with anger. He looked at Maria and shook his head. "It's your fault this girl is acting like this. You let her get away with more than the other girls because she's slow."

Anna hadn't been expecting this response. She turned to her mutti.

"Why do you have blood on your face?" Maria asked.

"Oh, that's from when I hit George with the lamp."

Her parents were open-mouthed now and almost at the same time said, "You go home right now and ask for forgiveness. It's not right for you to hit your husband. You are to obey him. You're bringing shame to our home and how we raised you. You will beg God and your husband for forgiveness at home." Anna's mutti was in the kitchen now, looking for a bowl. "You take this home to your husband for his dinner, and you stay there and care for him." She poured the stew into a bowl and handed it to her with a cloth wrapping. She looked her daughter in the eyes and pushed her toward the door.

Johan was holding the door open. "You do as your husband says. You don't come back here again, and if I hear about this from the elders or others, I will beat you myself. Get home." He pushed Anna out of the door and left her in the darkness of the street.

You didn't deserve that. George is not your boss, and you'll hit him again if he threatens you.

CHAPTER EIGHT: MARRIED LIFE IN MEXICO

Anna said, "Yes I will," and started walking home.

In the meantime, George had gone to see his vati and ask for his help. He saw the blood on his son's face, and when he heard what had happened, he was angry. "Don't let your wife do this to you. You're the man of the house, and you need to get it under control. You can't tell anyone what happened here. I raised you to be a man. Now you have to go be one."

"Vati, she won't listen to me. Today, she was lying in bed all day, didn't make my supper or breakfast, and was still in bed when I got home from work. When I told her to get out of bed, the look in her eyes was like a wild wolf, and she struck me."

"You keep her in line. You get the strap out and teach her how to act, to not bring shame on this family and your home. She'll soon learn what she has to do. Her parents should have raised her better, but now it's up to you to make sure she does what she's supposed to." His vati was afraid that word would get out in the colony and harm their name. He told his boy to tell others that a steer had caught him in the head and made the cut. There was no need to tell the truth.

Anna was walking home. Her face was sore; when she touched it, she winced. How could she have let the voices lead her to this? She knew what she had done was wrong, but she couldn't stop it. She didn't know how to manage the voices and do what was right. She had tried her whole life to be good, but she couldn't always follow the rules. Her dress was spotted with blood, and she wanted it off. She stopped at the side of the road and took it off. The voices guided her to be pure and leave the blood and devil thoughts behind. *Be pure.* She was naked now, but she didn't care. The dress was too dirty to be worn. It showed the failure she was and the shame she had for her behaviour.

She walked quietly home in the dark and through the front door of her house. The house was still in darkness, and she sat quietly in the corner, naked. She liked being invisible. The voices were less noisy, almost calming, when there was no one around her, and she longed for that.

It was very late when George came home. He'd had enough coaching from his vati to feel like he knew what had to be done for Anna. He walked through the door and saw Anna's eyes reflecting in the corner of the living room. She just sat and smiled at him. He felt a chill go across his neck as he looked at her. For a brief moment, he feared her, but he knew what he had to do to save his family's reputation and keep them from getting shunned.

"Get yourself out of that chair and get dressed. This is no way for a woman to be when their husband gets home. Get dressed and go to bed."

Anna was startled from her quiet meditative moment. She looked at him and followed his directions. "Supper is ready for you in the kitchen from my mutti," she said before going to get her nightdress on for bed.

She crawled into bed as she heard George in the kitchen, getting his plate out. That night, she felt that she should do what he said. She was exhausted. She had never been so tired in her mind or body. She crawled under the covers and was asleep before George came to bed.

He saw her in bed and crawled in next to her, lying on his side with his back to her and trying to sleep. He'd had moments where he was afraid of his wife and what she was capable of. Why had he not known that this was part of who she was? He had to do better as her husband, or he knew that his vati would beat him and then his wife until it was settled. He tried to sleep, and eventually, exhaustion took over, and he drifted off.

CHAPTER NINE:
GOD'S BLESSINGS

1960

The sun wasn't even up yet and George had been awakened by the sound of noise in the kitchen. He looked at his watch. It was already 4:30. It had been about two weeks since their quarrel, when Anna had run off to her parents. She'd had a few days in bed without getting up, and every day, George had taken off her covers and physically pushed her to get out of bed. It had been a struggle for both of them. But this morning was different. He could hear Anna in the kitchen as he started to get ready for the day.

He would start chores soon, so he dressed and walked to the kitchen. Anna was busy making breakfast and had the bread rising in the pans for the day's meals. He looked at her, and she gave him a small smile and put his food down for him.

This morning, Anna was awake and smiling. She patted her stomach. "I missed my monthly. In fact, I'm not really sure when I had my last one."

George looked at her, confused. The darkness in Anna's eyes from the weeks before was gone, and she looked more rested. "What are you saying?" he asked her in a flat tone.

She patted her stomach again. The voices were keeping her mind busy when she should have been noticing her round stomach and tiredness. God loved her, and He would protect her and this baby. George nodded acknowledgement to her announcement and ate his breakfast. She watched him eat the food that she

CHAPTER NINE: GOD'S BLESSINGS

had prepared, feeling proud of herself and this life they had. Everything was going to be okay.

George left that morning with a skip in his step as he walked out to his buggy and hitched the team up. He would be able to tell his vati and friends that he was going to be a vati himself and that he had successfully managed his wife. He could walk tall and proud that day.

Anna went about the morning chores.

You will be a perfect mutti.

It was the quiet, soft voice this time, so she found it comforting. If only George could understand her better. She had to make him understand that she had to do what the voices said. These were direct messages from God. If he knew and understood this, then he would be more patient with her. This baby would make them grow closer together and closer to God. She was happy, humming hymns to herself as she prepared the bread for its second rise before baking. She reached into her cabinet, behind the flour, and pulled out her bottle of alcohol she had hidden in the canning cupboard. She took a sip and smiled. The soothing burn was what had helped her through many days since childhood to stay calm and not worry as much.

"You must be submissive and make him happy," she said aloud. These were her mutti's words, but she had to learn to live by them. "Don't expect too much from him, and don't bother him with all the thoughts going through your head. That's what your sisters are for. Keep that in your family. Not everyone will understand your voices, so don't tell other women about it. You keep those thoughts for them. Don't bother your husband with all that." Anna would try her best to keep to these rules so she wouldn't be hit or hit back. She knew she could never do that again. She was excited to share her news about missing her monthlies and would have to see if she could get a ride to Campo 56 with a neighbour to let her family know. They would finally be proud of her. Her sisters had been having babies every year, and this was good for the colony and the church.

Anna waited outside after feeding the chickens to see if anyone was out with their buggy. She knew it was milk day and was hoping to get a ride on the wagon. She could see a cloud of red dust in the distance and waited. The sun was warm already, she knew what was for dinner, and the bread was already cooling from the oven on the countertop. She was ahead of herself.

You think you're special, don't you? Because you are special. Your husband loves you, and so do other men. It's up to you to share yourself with others, spread the word of God, and let Him know that you are doing His work.

Anna heard this in the soft voice and stopped for a moment to absorb the words and understand them like scripture. She was to be admired for her beauty, ability to bear children, and her handsome, hardworking husband. She would walk taller today in her five-foot frame because she had the direct support of God.

When the dust cleared, she could see a horse team and wagon. Johan, her soon-to-be brother-in-law, pulled up to the end of the lane with the wagon full of steel milk jugs. Anna ran toward him. "Are you going to Campo 56 today?" she asked. "I want to visit my parents."

"Yes, I can take you there, but I can't get you home. I'm only doing one run today."

Anna held her scarf tight around her hair and jumped onto the front bench of the wagon. Johan snapped the reins, and the horses went forward. She liked to be outside and feel the wind in her hair. It reminded her of being a young girl and playing in the mountains. When she was younger, she was afraid of the Mexicans, but now, she had a husband to protect her, and she knew that they were dirty and not her. She and Johan stopped at each farm with dairy cattle, and he loaded the steel cans onto the wagon behind the buggy. She was bursting to tell her mutti the news.

Anna watched him as she held her stomach. She found Johan handsome and was happy her sister Agatha would marry him in the next few months. She liked that he was strong and would make a good husband for her.

The milk would be taken to Cuauhtémoc to the cheese factory, and they would all get a bit of money from the sale of cheese. It took all of them to make a difference in the community. Crops were failing due to drought, so it was going to be a hard summer and winter with nothing canned or salted to eat in the months ahead.

"Here you go," Johan said and stopped the wagon.

"Thank you." Anna stepped down from the buggy and walked toward the house.

Her mutti was outside, taking laundry in, when she saw her approach. "I told you not to come back here. You stay home and look after your husband."

CHAPTER NINE: GOD'S BLESSINGS

Her mutti had anger in her voice as she stepped away from taking her clothes from the line.

Anna interrupted. "But mutti, I have good news. I'm with child. George is happy, and I made his meals and have bread ready for the day."

Anna's mutti stopped, looked at her daughter, and pulled her arm to get her into the house. "What are you talking about? You were just here a few weeks ago and made no mention of this." She reached her hand out to touch Anna's stomach and could feel the firmness of her abdomen under the pleats. She pulled her hand back, surprised. She was three or four months pregnant. "You don't tell anyone else. This is for you and your husband. Your sisters will know, but no one else. Right?"

Anna nodded. She really wanted to share her news and show other women in the colony that she was worthy of God's love. She had always been an outsider at church and hadn't been invited to many sewing or Bible reading groups. The fact that she was pregnant would help her fit in, and the other women would realize she was just like them. God loved her too, and the child was an example of how devoted she was to Him. She also knew from her voices that He approved of her, and that she would be a good mutti. God wouldn't give her a child if she was sinful and unworthy.

Maria gave a big sigh and then said, "We need to make your dresses bigger for you. Next time you come, we'll do some sewing and get things ready for the baby. Sit. You need to take care of the two of you now, but you also need to keep up your chores and home. It's not easy, but you get used to it."

Anna nodded with a smile on her face. She liked when her mutti gave her attention and made her feel special. She could do this the same as her sisters and friends.

Maria found an old apron to fit around Anna's dress and cover her growing stomach. Anna wasn't very tall, and carrying a baby would be hard to hide for very long. Maria reached her hands around Anna's waist to see if the apron ties were long enough. "That'll be good for a few months, and then I'll sew longer ties on it for you."

Anna beamed. She felt special, and her mutti wasn't mad at her. She didn't like it when everyone was mad at her. The voices in her head were reassuring too.

You are worthy of this gift from God.

"This baby is a gift from God," said Maria. "You must make sure you take care of it. You're in a partnership with God to make sure this baby is healthy and happy. You take care of it, and God will take care of both of you."

Anna nodded. She was smiling as she finished putting on the apron and twirled.

"When you're in the 'other time,' you need to get rest and do your work in the early hours of the day to keep the swelling down in your legs. You keep up the house and get some food put away for when the baby comes. You'll need to do your part even after. You'll know when it's time for the baby to come, and then you'll send George for me. I'll bring Susanna to help birth the baby. She's birthed many of them." Anna was still twirling in her apron, smiling. Maria took her arm to stop her. "Have the voices stopped, Anna? You need to stop the voices with prayer. Then, everything will be as God wants it."

Anna nodded, but she knew the voices were there to help, and she had no fear of what they might tell her to do.

Anna and her mutti and sisters never talked about pregnancy or birth. Sometimes at quilting gatherings or church meetings, the women would share stories of leg pains and back aches, but no one would dare mention this to their husbands. It wasn't their responsibility to worry about carrying a child or continuing on with the duties of the home. Anna had sat in on some of these meetings and learned bits and pieces of what it was like to be pregnant. She didn't know about labour but had helped with caring for her sisters' children when the birth occurred. The women silently shared knowledge with one another about pregnancy and birth to guide them through their struggles and tribulations. More words were unspoken than spoken, and ladies just nodded in support of the women's health concerns. You learned about sex from the pastor and your role to be submissive, but you never really understood the act or anatomy of how a child would be born. Anna counted on her mutti and sisters to teach her and lead her through this first pregnancy.

Maria was still thinking of how her daughter would cope with a baby and what items she might need when she said, "You'd better get home and put your dinner on now for George."

"Yes, mutti," said Anna, and then she proudly told her about the supper she already had planned for George, including *tweebak* and chicken *sup* (soup).

CHAPTER NINE: GOD'S BLESSINGS

Maria nodded. "I know that Susan next door is going to see her daughter soon. She can give you a ride home."

Anna went with Maria to the neighbours' and started to hitch up the horses. Anna crawled up to the buggy seat to ride with Susan home. She was just about to tell her about the pregnancy when she stopped. It was her secret, and she loved having one. The campo women never talked about being pregnant, and modesty and embarrassment kept them quiet; the women had their own secret terms for pregnancy ,Ondren tiet " another time" Their clothing would be adjusted constantly to hide the growing belly so others wouldn't know they were "in flower."

Despite that, Susan still knew by looking at Anna and the apron that she was pregnant.

Anna was home with ample time to get the house ready. She hadn't been working long in the kitchen when she heard the voices begin again. As she looked outside the window, a bright light shone on her. She squinted her eyes due to the brightness and heard clearly:

You deserve to be loved, and God loves you. You follow me, and I will lead you to eternal life.

She was sure that God himself was giving her this message. It made her take a deep breath in awe. How blessed she was to be able to hear Him directly and act as His servant. Not only was she pregnant, but God spoke to her directly. She was the chosen one. She smiled as she stood in the kitchen with the sun setting, feeling the power of God and knowing that she was chosen to bear this child.

As she collected her eggs for the next day, Anna reached behind the steel feed bin and took out one of her bottles. It was common to have a few bottles hidden in different places for a drink when it was needed. She had learned from her mutti and a few other women to save some isopropyl alcohol from the chemist. A small number of pesos could buy enough alcohol to mix and sip for a month or more. She'd added sugar and fruit juices to make it taste more palatable, and because she knew her mutti and her sisters did the same thing, she didn't feel that God would punish her for this bit of relief for the nerves. She enjoyed a sip when she needed to be calm. It burned as it went down, but it helped her relax.

Drinking wasn't approved by the elders, but Anna had been drinking since she was a young girl, and many of her friends did the same. After church, the youth would all gather to talk and meet other girls and boys, and often, they shared a small jar of alcohol between them as they socialized away from the adults. Her parents were also drinking throughout Anna's upbringing, and George also was witness to the secret jar that his parents both filled and emptied. Having a drink throughout the day helped Anna to make her daily duties more manageable and took the edge off her voices. She could think clearer with a few drinks. It was her little treat. She rubbed her swollen stomach as she took a second gulp from the bottle and put it back in the hiding spot.

CHAPTER TEN:
THE BIRTH

1960

Anna felt some lower back pain, which wasn't unusual at this late stage of her pregnancy. She had been doing well, and even after a full day of housework and gardening, her ankles weren't swollen. The pregnancy brought pride from her parents, friends, and most of all from her husband. She was finally looked upon with approving eyes at church too. No one would speak of the pregnancy, but everyone silently knew. Her sisters had some concerns with her being slow and managing a house and children. They spoke of these concerns between themselves but never to Anna.

Anna was hearing the voices less now, and she was happy about it. Whenever they did come, they reinforced how divine she was and how she would be bringing forth the best, most beautiful babies as given to her by the Lord. The voices also told her that other men longed for her because of her looks and how easily she carried her baby; she didn't like these last voices because they made her long for other men, and this was forbidden by the word of God.

She was keeping on top of her house chores and had even been making a few friends so she could have tea with others while her husband worked. Pregnancy drew women together, even if it wasn't discussed. Everyone knew the struggles ahead and what would be needed. Everyone but Anna. She hadn't been part of anyone's birth or preparation, and she wasn't sure what to expect or plan for.

CHAPTER TEN: THE BIRTH

Her sister Agatha was her best friend, but she lived several campos away, and getting to see her was hard if George had taken the team out.

That day, she hung out her wash and had some nausea and exhaustion. She had never been this tired before. As she reached above her head to hang out the tea towels, she felt a sharp pain in her lower abdomen. It made her catch her breath, and she lunged forward to hold her stomach. She breathed through the pain and then continued hanging out the clothes. Again, she felt the sharp pain, and it made her worry. Was it time for the baby? She knew that she was big enough, but it was a bit early. The pains continued, and she went next door to get her neighbour, Agathena, to ask her to take her to her mutti's.

"You will have all day of this," Agathena said. "It's your first. I'll go after I make my dinner for the family. Best thing to do is keep working. Take big breaths, and just focus on the work. It makes the baby come faster."

Anna doubled over with a contraction as Agathena was telling her this. "But it's very sore. How can I work? What if the baby comes?"

Agathena smiled. "It gets a bit easier with each one." She looked outside to her children playing. "This will be the one that takes the longest. Go home. After my baking is ready, I'll fetch your mutti."

Anna was shocked that Agathena wouldn't help her considering how much pain she was in. She started to walk home and had four contractions on her way. There was so much dust in the air, and they really needed rain. On those days, the wind would pick up, and the air would be red with soil. She tried to breathe deeply with each contraction, taking in a mouth of red dirt at the same time. She could feel the panic building inside her. What did Agathena know? Anna had been getting messages directly from God and knew that she was more special than any other woman in the campo.

Anna went home and started supper, her mutti's words in her ears. *It's your job, no matter what, to make dinner and have babies. Keep doing your work.* Anna tried, but she couldn't focus. The voices returned.

The baby is sick. You're killing the baby. Lay down.

Her heart raced, and panic rose again. She was sweating and trying to stay calm, but God was telling her other things. She didn't know what to do and started to run, holding her lower abdomen. She ran into Agathena's adobe home without knocking, and Agathena was just sitting at the table, taking the ends off the green beans for their dinner. Her eyes shot up when she saw Anna.

"What's wrong? Why are you here now?"

"God says something is wrong. I know something is wrong. It hurts too much. I need to have the baby out now." Anna was panting and yelling, and her pupils were pinpoint. She was in full panic.

Agathena lifted Anna's dress to see if she had blood or water on her legs or stockings. She was trying to understand if this was coming faster. She'd had a dozen kids of her own and knew it could feel very painful but still take days. Anna was running in circles again when the next contraction came, yelling loudly.

"God is coming for my baby. I need to get it out. I need to get it out."

Agathena and her children stood around her as she yelled. She spoke to her oldest girl. "You watch the kids and finish the supper. I'm going to take Anna to her mutti." Her daughter nodded with wide eyes as she corralled all the children into the yard, telling them to stop watching Anna. Agathena quickly got the horses ready and latched and hooked the buggy up. "Anna, stop your running and yelling. You'll hurt the baby. Get in the buggy, now."

Anna couldn't focus on the words. She only knew that her job and commitment to God was to keep this baby safe, and now, things weren't going as planned. She felt Agathena's hand on her arm and reactively slapped it away.

"Shhh. Anna, get in the wagon. We'll go and have your baby."

Anna nodded just as another contraction came. It dropped her to her knees, and she gave a primal yell that made the kids all turn in fear. When the contraction ended, Agathena helped Anna to the buggy, and she stepped up to the seat. Agathena was embarrassed and hoped that no one near her home had heard the screams. Mennonite women laboured quietly. It was their suffering and gift to bear. They didn't scream like this for others except maybe their sisters or mutti to hears.

Agathena took the reins and whipped the horse. She was watching Anna and feared she would jump from the buggy if it was too slow. She was timing the contractions by counting each one, and it seemed like the baby was a long way from coming. She had heard of women who lost their minds during labour, but most kept this fear inside. It wasn't like a woman to be this loud and vocal, which made her worry that the baby might have turned and was feet first or that there would be problems with the afterbirth. She thought this silently to

CHAPTER TEN: THE BIRTH

herself, as she knew that sharing any information with Anna would make her unable to continue labour and have a healthy baby.

They arrived at Anna's mutti's home to find her in the garden feeding chickens. As the buggy stopped, Anna jumped off and ran toward her mutti, screaming. Maria rose from the earth and saw her daughter holding her abdomen and running toward her. She looked into Anna's eyes and saw only black circles.

"The baby is coming, the baby is coming," Anna yelled, panting.

Agathena and Maria exchanged glances, and Maria grabbed her arm. "Shhh. Come into the house now. No more yelling." Agathena asked if she was needed, and Maria shook her head no. "Could you get the midwife down the road to come down?" Agathena agreed and got into her buggy to bring back the midwife, Susanna.

"The baby is coming," Anna yelled again as another contraction started. Maria told her to stop yelling, but a contraction came, and Anna screamed, loud and long.

Maria slapped her across the face. "Stop that. You go into the house and stop this yelling. God will take care of the baby. You need to do your work by taking the pain."

Anna was startled. How could her mutti slap her when she was in pain? She raised her arm to hit her back and then tucked it tightly against her side. She had to stop hitting. "The baby needs to come out. God says so."

Maria shook her head. "Oh, Anna, you're a long way from having this baby. You need to listen to your mutti and Susanna, and then you'll have your baby. It may not be today, but you have to be quiet. The men don't need to hear this yelling. You're not special. We all have experienced this." Susanna arrived, and Agathena waited for a bit before heading home to her children. Maria knew that it was going to be a hard birth for Anna.

As Susanna walked in, she asked, "Have your waters broken? Is there any blood?"

"No, I don't think so," said Anna. She had no idea what that meant. Another contraction came, and she yelled again. Both Maria and Susanna looked at each other. They knew it would be a long day. Anna was bouncing and yelling. Susanna had helped birth many babies in the colony, but she hadn't had very many that acted out like this during labour. It made her startle.

Anna yelled again, "I need to get the baby out."

When the contraction was over, Susanna sat Anna down and laid her back on the floor. "Let me examine you." She reached under her skirt, and Anna screamed again. She had no idea why the midwife put fingers inside her. She felt dirty and sinful, which made her hold her thighs closer together. Susanna said, "You're only two fingers open. You have many hours left. Even your waters are intact." They moved her to the barn so the men could have their supper.

Over the course of the day and into the night, Anna was running in circles, intermittently laying on the ground and panting in the barn. Her water had broken, so there was more risk of the cord getting compressed. Susanna, Maria, and other colony women walked her to the egg sorting table and laid her down. Anna continued to have contractions, and they used a rope to tie her to the table, first tying her legs and then one arm. It was the only way to keep her there. Susanna had done this once before to make sure the baby would stay safe until it was time. Shortly after being restrained, Anna started grunting and pushing.

Eighteen hours after the first pain, Anna delivered a baby girl. The women cleaned Anna and the baby as she closed her eyes and slowed her breathing down and tried to understand everything that she had just been through. They were all exhausted. Chickens clucked in the background as the women wrapped her new daughter in a cloth and cleaned the afterbirth and fluid with the straw from the barn floor. They untied Anna from the table when they finished cleaning and checking her bleeding, encouraging her to sit up.

They pinned rags at the front and back of Anna's dress to hold the pad in place for the blood. They helped her up for a drink and some bread. She eagerly drank. She looked around for her baby, and they handed it to her. She smiled, and the baby looked back at her with dark eyes. She had tufts of black hair, and Anna unwrapped her and counted her fingers and toes. She was perfect. God was right. She would have a perfect baby. She felt soreness between her legs as she sat up. The women prepared more rags for her to take home with her and helped her to the ground. Anna moaned with pain and exhaustion as she walked out of the barn, holding her new daughter.

George had been on his way to the farm to see his new child, and he would take Anna home. He was at the house and walked over to see her. He opened the blanket around the baby and saw his daughter's little face looking at him. His first child. God was good. He smiled at her and patted Anna on the shoulder before helping them into the buggy and taking his family home.

CHAPTER ELEVEN:
MOTHERHOOD

1960–1964

Anna initially had a hard few days at home. She had only five days after her daughter, Gertruda (named after George's mutti), was born to recover. Some women had help for three to four days at home after giving birth with meals and doing the laundry but her mutti was too far away to care for her, and her sisters' girls were also too far away. She learned to cope by listening to the word of God in her head. She was still getting her personal messages from Him, and late at night, she could hear Him more clearly.

Her neighbours and mutti had brought baking and were washing rags and blankets to keep Anna and her new daughter clean. As time went on, she was able to get up and do her baking and keep the laundry caught up. She wasn't sleeping well, which made the voices in her head louder. She tried hard not to listen to them and just focus on her baby.

Anna was nursing her baby in the night. It had been four months, and Gertruda was growing just perfectly. Still, Anna would look into her dark eyes and worry if she would be a good enough mutti. In the middle of the night, it was quiet, and nothing else was expected of her. During the day, everything was overwhelming. Keeping the house, animals, and yard maintained, as well as pleasing her husband and having his dinner ready, was exhausting.

You know you are God's creature, and you are following the path of righteousness as laid out in the Bible.

CHAPTER ELEVEN: MOTHERHOOD

Anna would answer yes, sometimes out loud, other times in her head. He could hear her words, just like she could hear His without speaking them aloud. The baby cried a lot, and Anna found herself going to the chicken coop for drinks more than usual. After a few weeks and minimal sleep, Anna finally regained more energy. She was able to keep up with cooking and cleaning and even found that she really didn't need much sleep. Despite her fears, she felt she was better than many other muttis in raising children. They complained about being exhausted, but Anna seemed to be able to do it with no sleep now. The voices guided her. Mostly, they were good voices, but when the bad voices came, she found comfort in her bottle. It soothed her mind and nerves. She could have some days of so much energy and happiness, and then just as fast, she was exhausted, living in darkness and doubting about her abilities to live this life. It seemed that this phase of darkness would never end, and then a few weeks later, she was again happy and euphoric to be a mutti and wife.

Anna had another baby seven months later, Jacob. She had this baby at home. This pregnancy went quicker, and her labour was less of a surprise. She used chloroform for this birth to sedate herself. One of the birthing ladies had some, and since Anna had had so many struggles with her first child, she decided she would use the medication. It didn't make the labour shorter, but she remembered less of it. She was still tied down, and the midwife prayed during the labour as Anna faded in and out of consciousness. Her mutti was there and held her arms across her Anna's shoulders to keep her in the bed. She had her oil cloth from the table ready under her hips and sheets and rags ready for the delivery. She felt more in control this time. She could hear the praying and felt God all around her. He was in her head and in the room.

This child will also be a blessing chosen just for you. You are very special, and you will have the most beautiful children.

By the time Jacob was born, Anna had stopped nursing Gertruda to nurse him instead. Jacob looked at her with such curiosity. He had the blackest hair and dark eyes, and she liked that her children looked like her. She was created in the eyes of God, and her children looked just like her, so this meant they were holy as well. George was pleased to welcome his first son, but he himself was blonde and blue-eyed, so having dark-haired children made him wonder sometimes about the vati of these children. But he knew that his wife's family had this colouring, so it put his mind to rest.

After Anna had her second child, life became hard again. She couldn't keep up. Where she thrived on little sleep with her first baby, this second baby made it impossible to rest. She was falling behind in the baking and washing, and often, she was sleeping when George came in from the fields. After Jacob, George had the neighbour send over their daughter to help. This allowed Anna time to get things done around the house because Gertruda was crawling around into everything now. Sometimes, Anna's sisters would send one of their girls over for a few weeks to help with the cooking and cleaning. George knew Anna wasn't keeping up like other women in the colony, and he wasn't afraid to tell her. They still had to be pressed and ready for church. Keeping face in front of the elders and colony was important to ensure your family wasn't talked about. Women would try and help out, but they had so many of their own children that in the end, it was a lonely process of learning, coping, and reproducing.

George Jr. was born one year to the day that she had birthed Jacob. He was in his vati's likeness, and all worry about who the vati was vanished. He had blonde hair and blue eyes, and he was a big baby, over ten pounds. Anna was relieved to make her husband happy with another son. She was doing God's work and giving children to the world.

You are worthy of my blessings. You are making God's perfect children, and you are my perfect child, the voices would tell her in the night.

She needed the reassurance from her voices and her bottle because her husband and parents were ashamed of how she was unable to keep everything running like a good housewife. She rarely had time to wash and comb or braid her hair. She couldn't remember when she bathed the babies last. The clothes were too small for the babies, and she had no time to mend them or make more. The girls that came in to help out often brought clothes from their homes to put on the children. Anna still made bread, but sometimes at three or four in the morning, which made George angry, as it woke up the babies. Anna was sleeping less with each child.

Anna was drinking more frequently. She was making alcohol but would also get it from any kids she knew or from Mexicans when she was in town. When her nieces were over helping her with the house, she would send them to the chemist for alcohol with a bit of money and a jar. The chemist would always ask the children what it was for, and they would just shrug. He would give a bit from his large jar in the office, and they would go back to Anna.

CHAPTER ELEVEN: MOTHERHOOD

George was struggling to get enough money to put food on the table. He was working for the Mexicans in the fields now, as the crops that the colony had planted failed again due to drought. Working for the Mexicans was frowned upon by the church, and any time spent with them was seen as turning your back on God. He also started getting bottles from the Mexicans as part of his pay. He kept his bottle in the buggy under the seat, just like all his friends. He knew it was wrong, but the elders already knew many of the colony were drinking. As long as it was kept quiet, they would let it go.

He would come home and find Anna smelling of sweat, yeast from baking, and dried breast milk. His children weren't clean, and he often only spoke with the daughter from the colony who was caring for his children. He couldn't wait to go out of the house to work every day to be free of the madness. His vati told him how to make things work better at home, but he was too tired to listen, exhausted from keeping Anna in line. All he could really hope for was that on Sunday, they looked good in the eyes of the colony.

The voices weren't always supportive of Anna.

You can do better than this. Look at Katarina next door. She has eight children and keeps a tidy house. You're worthless.

Anna cried when she heard these words and yell back, "I'm as good as she is. I am. I do my best, and my babies are prettier and nicer than hers."

When Anna went to church on Sunday, other muttis would look at her across the rows and whisper. She knew that they were judging her and felt that they were all against her. At least she sometimes saw a familiar face in her sisters and mutti at church. She did very little with the other women in the campo. She didn't need their judgement, and her inner God told her to watch them.

You're prettier than those girls, and you have the most handsome husband.

She looked across the church to the men's side and saw her husband there with his brothers and brothers-in-law. Her own brother, Gerhard, sat next to him. Even with the years going by, their friendship was very important to them, and they were hardly ever seen apart. They loved farming and the work. Even though it was hard sometimes with no rain and crops not coming in as they had hoped, they got through it together.

Anna smiled to herself in the church pew. She knew that others were jealous, and she also knew that having God speak just to her was something so very special and not meant for everyone. She was the chosen one, and she would keep this to herself. This pride made her sit up taller. She would stand tall and try harder. She looked at her children with pride. The voices in her head from God helped her remember that she was more special than others. She had brought these children of God into the world, and she was blessed. Church had always been a place of gathering, but also judgement on the cleanliness of the clothing, the whiteness of the whites, and even how the horses were being fed and cared for.

Anna went home on this Sunday to prepare their food. Often on Sundays, families came over and kids played, and she was hoping to be part of this. She knew other ladies in the campo were baking, and she had already prepared her faspa. Her kids were running and crawling. George Jr. was still breastfeeding, but she knew it was hard to keep him full, so she was putting pablum in bottles for him too. Her milk wasn't as plentiful with this baby.

Anna had days where her mood was very low. She slipped into darkness, and her body was so heavy that she couldn't lift it out of bed. The girls who came to help would do all her chores, and she would just lay down. They would go back and tell their muttis about Anna, and this kept her further away from them. Women had to keep a family together, and if they couldn't, the judgement from others would keep them down. No helping hand was given to lift them up. Everyone was just surviving. Some days, she could hardly get up in the morning, making George very angry.

"Other women are making meals and keeping a house. You should be doing the same. It's not my job to help you with this. I work outside and bring home our food. I can't help you. If you need help, go to your mutti and sisters, and maybe they can send someone over to help you. We have no money to pay, but you could bake for them. Get out of bed." George was getting frustrated with the pressure he felt from the men in the colony and the ministers about making sure Anna did her role. He pulled on her arm to get her out of bed, and she fell to the floor. She was so groggy from lack of sleep, but lying there, she could hear the babies crying.

George kicked her in the hip to get her off the floor, and she winced. "Get up and look after your children. I need to work for the Mexicans today to get us food. You know how hard that is, working for them when I really want my own land and farm. We're all having hardships."

CHAPTER ELEVEN: MOTHERHOOD

He stomped down the hallway, and she could hear him getting his breakfast. She blinked several times before focusing.

You should kick him back. He has no right to do this to you.

She didn't have the energy to address George and listened with confidence to the voices. She slowly got to her knees and went to the babies. She set Gertruda down from her crib and changed her diaper, then Jacob's. They shared the same crib. She cleaned them and then got to George Jr. She sat in the chair to nurse him as the others ran about. George Jr. was one now. She was still submitting to her husband, but there was no baby, and this wasn't good in the eyes of God.

She put on a pot of water to boil for laundry and piled the dirty diapers on the floor. The pile was now almost to her knees. The smell was pungent as she started to make some bread and eggs for the children and focus on the day. There were days like this where it was only darkness in her eyes and soul. She didn't know why. She knew that her legs were heavier, and her heart was not kind or forgiving. She didn't like being a mutti on these days. She drank more to help ease her worry and the voices in her head.

You're not good at being a mutti. You weren't even meant to be a mutti. You don't care enough, keep them clean enough, or feed them enough.

She could tell the children didn't like her either. They played away from her, and when the neighbour sent her daughter over to help Anna when there had been no wash on the line for a couple of days, they loved her more.

Anna put the wash into the boiling water with their whitewash from the chemist. She boiled the diapers to get them clean and washed all the other clothing in the steel washbasins. When the wash was white, she hung them out on the line. Even though it took all her energy to do the laundry on these days, she found pleasuring in seeing the long clothesline full of clean clothes.

At least you can do this right, said her inner voice.

Anna forced a grin. He was right. She could. The days of darkness made the voices hate her. She hated to hear them, and she couldn't get them to stop. She covered her ears and sang hymns, but they continued. She wanted to yell at them, but the babies and anyone around could hear her. She would sometimes go out to the garden and use the hoe to take out her frustrations on the soil and plants. Once, she took down a whole row of green beans and didn't even remember it. She just wanted it to stop and to have silence again.

Whenever her kids cried, it was the worst, piercing sound to her. She would slap them to make them stop, but they would just cry more, so she would leave them soiled in their cribs until she had the strength to come in and face them again. After a few weeks of dark days, the sun came out again. She got her energy back and enjoyed her work at home. She had supper ready for George, and they even shared a few laughs. It was hard work supporting her husband because he was struggling to find enough work to feed everyone. When she and the kids were dirty and crying, it only made their relationship harder. George looked forward to the sunny days too, when his wife would be ready at home and life seemed normal in the eyes of God.

Anna was so happy to feel a baby kick inside her stomach again. She was blessed and able to hold her head up high again, and the voices were kind to her.

You're amazing. Look at how perfect you are when you're pregnant. This baby will be the best yet. God is on your side.

Anna could walk with pride. She liked being up early to get the house ready, and sometimes, she never even went to bed. She baked, washed, and cleaned. George was smiling at her when he got up in the morning. She was being the wife her mutti and congregation would be proud of. She felt her best when she was with child, worthy of God and her congregation. George was in charge of the how things ran in the home, and Anna respected that. She didn't try to change anything but just did her jobs, even though in her head, she knew some of her jobs should have been done by a man.

Don't say anything. Just do the work.

This echoed in her head as she milked the cows with the kids crawling on the barn floor and running. She would make sure her kids were brought up right. Her own upbringing had been hard. There had been starvation and fighting, and her vati, Johan, had died young of too much drinking. She stood up from the milking stool and put a hand to her lower back. With each pregnancy, she was feeling the aches and pains earlier.

The Mexican government liked that Anna and her family were having lots of babies. They wanted more people of mixed races, and if she was lucky, she would have a blonde child again, like George Jr. The Mexicans like the blondes because it was so different from their own people.

Anna would have a quick labour and birth this time, but the baby would be very small. He came too early and looked like a spider with all the veins

CHAPTER ELEVEN: MOTHERHOOD

running through him. He wouldn't latch on and died within two days. God was punishing Anna for her drinking, bad thoughts, and dirty home. This was the proof she and her husband needed. The next baby girl they had also died, the crops all failed, and the campo was in a bad way, trying to keep their faith. Mexican bandits were coming into the colony to take back land, raping any women that they could find and stealing what few things that the Mennonites had. The elders went to the government to ask for help with keeping their land and people safe. The government sent armed guards to help them. This was the last thing many wanted.

Things were getting harder for the Mennonites of Cuauhtémoc. The crops weren'ts growing because of their old ways of farming. Their Old Colony values made sure they didn't have tractors and machinery, so they couldn't survive as others were. Just a few campos over, they had tractors, plows, and irrigation, and they were making a very good living.

For weeks, George had been hoeing beets and picking watermelons for other farmers and some Mexicans. He would take Anna and the kids with him to work so they could pick more fruit. Anna could have a wood fire in the fields and make tortillas to eat with the melon. The sun was hot, and the children couldn't work long days. It was hard for everyone.

Working off the campo with and for Mexicans was necessary for survival, but it also caused a lot of tension with the elders. Working with the Mexicans opened George up to other ideas away from the work of his colony and God. The elders of the Old Colony Mennonites weren't progressive where George lived; even working with Mennonites from different campos could lead to shunning. He was thinking of how he could do more to be successful for his family, but he also was developing resentment toward the elders and pastors for holding back his progress.

George would often be angry when he got home from work. "The Mexicans are bad people, but they can feed their families. They drive trucks and tractors, but we can't even put rubber wheels on our buggy. We can't get ahead this way. No one is helping us, and yet we see that others are doing well and still going to church." His resentment built when he saw what other colonies were doing, but when he talked it over with the elders, they shook their heads no. It brought more questions about his faith than wishes for a progressive farm. They told him that if he prayed more and showed God he was devoted, he would get a better crop.

George began to speak to his friends about immigrating to Ontario. Many Mexicans he worked for had gone as migrant workers to Ontario in the summer to earn extra money. George thought that if he did this too, he would get enough money to buy his own farm in Mexico. He had several family members making their journey back to Canada, and they were starting to get ahead and buying land. He was born in Mexico, but his grandparents were from Manitoba, and they sold all their good farms to move here.

In 1920, before his grandparents' migration to Mexico, they had to sell all their farms to come up with enough money to buy the land in Mexico. Some farmers did well with the sales, and others were left taking half the amount so they wouldn't miss the train. When the voice of religious freedom is voiced by the elders and pastor, the congregation follows. It wasn't about personal property, but the religious freedom to teach their children in their way to sustain their culture and beliefs. Fear and protectionism of their heritage would drive this move to foreign lands yet again.

As George made plans for his family to go to Ontario as migrant workers, Anna delivered a healthy, happy baby girl named Maria. She was blonde and blue-eyed, with the whitest skin. Anna was so proud of her. She was her first blonde baby girl, and she was perfect.

George was busy getting money together for the move to Canada. Some of the Mennonite men were going off of the colony and working for the Mexicans, but they weren't paid reliably, and sometimes, they were given alcohol instead of money for flour. The Mennonites weren't used to drinking and often consumed too much of what they were paid with and spent many hours laying in the fields, earning no money. Other Mennonite families were moving to Paraguay to get their own land and start another colony to live their conservative ways.

It would take several months before they had enough money to buy a car. George was excited to own his first car, and he had Mexicans helping him find one and making sure it would run well to make the trip. He would get a ride to Chihuahua and buy his first Oldsmobile that would take him to Canada, as they couldn't take the buggy.

CHAPTER TWELVE:
MIGRANT WORKERS IN ONTARIO

1966

George and Anna wouldn't be alone in travelling to Canada or living there. Another couple drove with them, and Anna's brother Gerhard and sister-in-law Margaret were expecting them in Port Burwell, Ontario. There would be jobs in the fields for them when they arrived and a temporary house until they could save enough for their own. They finally had hope again, even as Anna was working through the grief of losing two children and burying them in Mexico.

Not all the children were walking yet. Gertruda wasn't learning as fast as other children at Sunday school. She didn't speak as much, and they thought she was going to be a bit slow. Jake was quiet but could play and talk. George Jr. just followed his older brother and copied everything his father did.

George was trying hard to bring home more money. All these children needed food, and he could see how thin they were at the weekly bath. George needed to make some decisions about how to provide food and get ahead. Other Mennonite farmers were prospering that had made the move to Canada. They had money to buy land, the equipment needed to maintain it, and the means of irrigating it. He was jealous of them, even though he knew it was wrong. The ones who had money would lend money to others but charge very high

CHAPTER TWELVE: MIGRANT WORKERS IN ONTARIO

interest rates, and if the crops failed, they would take back the land. It was hard to survive in Mexico, but they had hopes that it would be better in Canada.

They travelled with the other family for twelve days from Cuauhtémoc, Mexico to Port Burwell, Ontario. George and his escort didn't want to stop on the way to Ontario, so he filled the car with food and his four children and Anna. George couldn't speak English, so asking for help or anything else was going to be hard for him. He would bring enough gas cans to take him almost to Ontario. He had never been outside of Mexico and had heard stories of being robbed and the types of people to watch for. In fear, he decided to avoid as many people as possible, hold all of his money in his pocket, and closely watch his belongings.

The man they had hired to transport them to Ontario and take care of them on their arrival was greedy. They had gotten his name from another Mennonite family already working in Ontario. He spoke Plautdietsch and English and would help them with translating at the borders between Mexico and USA, as well as USA and Canada. He had promised them many things, including escorting them to their new homes, in return for most of the money they had from selling their belongings to other Mennonite families. When they crossed the USA border, the driver did all the talking. On the journey, they often slept in the car, taking turns sleeping during the day. It was hot, and the kids were sick to their stomachs. No one had ever been in a car before. They stopped at gas stations to wash the kids and clean the car out, but the smell of vomit was in the seats and the air for the entire trip to Ontario.

When they arrived, the driver arranged a home, but it was falling apart. The roof was open to the air in sections, and over half the windows were broken. It was much cooler in Ontario than Mexico, and it rained a lot more. They lived within the house, trying to find areas to stay dry while taking in their surroundings. The house had to be shared by six more families. They were all hopeful but scared of what might come. The home was on a farm, and at one point, it would have provided a lovely space for a large family. Disrepair and the lack of tenants for several years had left it falling down.

The Mennonites in the area and farmers helped the families by bringing food to them until they got their first paycheques. They acted as interpreters for them as they started to learn English. As more rental accommodations became available, one by one, each family was matched with a home where they could spend the summer.

The average workday was from 8 a.m. to 6 p.m. for everyone that was over the age of six. The family, even the younger ones, all worked in the fields, picking cucumbers, tomatoes, peppers, and tobacco for their livelihood. The conditions were harsh, exposed to weather and with limited access to water and food. The families were against sending their children to school, as they needed the extra hands in the field to make more money. Most schools in the colonies were run by men, but most teaching in Ontario was by women, which wasn't seen as favourable by Mennonites.

Never in the history of the Mennonite people had they been living amid regular people of the world, where their children were asked to attend provincially run schools. It was a time of resistance, fear, and uncertainty. If school attendants were rumoured to be making rounds to Mennonite homes, word would get out, and children would be hidden, especially the girls, who were needed to provide childcare for their families to keep them all working.

After a few weeks in the fields picking vegetables, George was able to find work picking tobacco. Their driver from Mexico, also a Mennonite, worked as the foreman and garnished their wages to pay for travel and food expenses for the trip, as well as his own expenses, with a profit for himself. Since the farmer paid him directly, George was left with just enough money to buy bread. He couldn't afford meat or anything else. It was hard to fill children's stomachs with just bread, and Anna had no flour or corn to make tortillas until a few weeks after George started working. The Old Colony Mennonite Church and Mennonite Central Committee worked with the new families to get them clothing and food basics to survive, but it was still difficult to feed the family.

There was no breast milk for the babies, but she had to nurse Maria and George to help them keep their weight on. Anna hadn't been eating well and had been working in the fields with her family, so she had lost weight and wasn't getting enough nutrition to keep producing breast milk. Nursing so many babies was hard on Anna, and her teeth were starting to fall out. As migrant workers on visas, they weren't entitled to healthcare, so being sick and missing a day of work was unthinkable. The living facilities were damp and unpleasant, but they had heard from their pastor and other families that signing up for welfare payment from the government meant that eventually, the government

CHAPTER TWELVE: MIGRANT WORKERS IN ONTARIO

would control everything they did, how they would live, and who to worship. This fear was enough to keep them all suffering to earn what they could. As bad as the conditions might have been, it didn't match the lack of money and food in Mexico, where there was no hope for anything better.

Not enough milk for all of you, so the mother gives up her bones and teeth to make more echoed in Anna's head from the voices of other Mennonite women as she put pressure on her jaw to control the bleeding.

This time of stress and chaos made the voices in Anna's head talk twenty-four hours a day. She used to be able to sit very still to hear them, but now, there was never a time when it was quiet enough. They had started yelling at her. Sometimes, the voices would come out of a dark corner or space, appearing in a cloak or robe that looked like something she imagined the devil would wear. They were real to her, but no one else seemed alarmed by their appearance.

You deserve the best in your life. Your husband isn't a good provider. You deserve a new one.

Anna knew that this wasn't right, so she would shake her head no when those suggestions came. She shook her head no so hard that she would fall over occasionally. She tried to do other things so she would not hear them.

The migrant workers were having a hard time providing for their families and finding work. Their contracts were arranged before their arrival, but with weather changes and crop delays, there were times when they weren't needed on the farms. This included George. He was trying as hard as he could to learn the English language, as he often saw bills of money being exchanged in front of him between whispering farm managers. He was sure they weren't paying any of them fairly. He was working alongside Mexicans that he used to work with in Mexico. This made him feel like he was back in the campo, fighting for his rights. He resented that he was being put side by side with them when other white men were running the farms and had positions of more authority. He would never treat them poorly, but it was a defeating feeling when you had visions of progress and it instead felt like he had never left the red soil behind.

When the men were stressed, they would buy rye whiskey from local farmers and drink in the fields before coming home. They knew it was frowned upon by the church, but it helped ease the disappointment of not being a good provider and not understanding the language and customs of this new country, where it was supposed to be better. George would try and fit in with the immigrant workers from Ontario, Quebec, and Mexico by having some drinks with them after work. Anna could smell the booze on him when he got home, and she shamed him for it.

"You're not a big enough man to work a full day, feed your family, and put a roof over our head, and now you spend your money on drink. God is ashamed of you, and so am I." Anna knew that challenging George was wrong, but the chaos was too much.

George was making about $1.38 per hour, or $13 per day, and he could see the driver taking more of his money and working less. Talk in the greenhouses was that they could move to another farm and work with housing in Aylmer, Ontario and get better pay. One night, after George had learned enough English and had made some acquaintances, they packed up the kids and found a farmer to drive them to another greenhouse that was looking for workers. The farmers provided a small home to George and Anna. It only had two rooms and an outside toilet, but it was dry and would be somewhere to start. It had housed chickens for the farmer for many years before being converted into living quarters for a family. It wasn't a house that either of them had ever lived in, with red insulbrick, wooden floors, and an electric stove. The walls were uninsulated, with no toilet and no electricity.

Other Old Colony Mennonites from the area collected clothing, a bed, a table, and a few chairs for them. There were two Mennonite churches familiar to them from Mexico in the area. Most were former members of the Old Colony church in Mexico and part of the group who organized these in Ontario. They were happy to be able to see others who had been down their path and were now making a good life. They did notice that the Old Colony members were using cars and trucks and had electricity and phones. They also didn't dress in a conservative way as they were raised in Mexico. Anna tried hard to perform the same role as a wife in Ontario as in Mexico, but she didn't have a neighbour to talk to.

The Mennonite Central Committee in Aylmer didn't support the formation of these churches without leadership and direction from a minister from Manitoba. He preached that "it's what's on the inside that matters, not so much how you look." This was controversial for the times, but some of the families were ready to conform to more modern dress and society. Others were not. George and Anna were eager to be part of this more moderate church, where

CHAPTER TWELVE: MIGRANT WORKERS IN ONTARIO

there were the possibilities of owning land, having a tractor, and then being more competitive with other families in Ontario and Mexico.

George and many of his friends had never owned their own farms in Mexico, and they were excited at the thought of doing this. They already knew of Mennonites who had saved enough money to go back home, buy farmland, and have a better life. He really wanted to get enough money and go back to Mexico at the end of the work visa to buy a farm near his father and brothers. It was his home, where he felt independent and free.

Anna, on the other hand, felt lost, as she couldn't understand English and didn't have a horse and buggy anymore. In the campo, she could be independent and visit friends or go to the stores with her own team. When they moved to Canada with the car, George had said that they would keep it and that there was no need to follow the old ways, but they couldn't afford the gasoline to go any farther than his work. Anna needed to meet other women to talk with because when she'd moved, her sisters didn't come with her. She was alone, and it was hard to endure with four children in a tiny home and no garden or animals to care for.

On the first Sunday with the new minister, they listened to his words about how God was watching over them. He told them that they must not stray from the word of God or fall to temptation. George knew these words were for him. He wasn't going back to the old ways of horse and buggy. He had seen cars and knew that farmers who succeeded used tractors. His views were changing, and so was he.

Anna knew that God was watching her. She could hear Him in her head, but His words weren't kind. She suspected that everyone was watching her and her children too. Wherever she went, people turned to look at her and whisper. She knew her kids were thin and dirty, yet she didn't have a way to fix it. She washed what she could, but with only one gas burner to heat water for laundry and to cook food, it was difficult. She was trying to make more things, but without familiar ingredients, she was left with store-bought things. Finding a balance between her Mexican ways and her new Ontario life was hard. She spent many days working in the fields all alone with no one to talk to but her children. When she worked in the fields all day, everyone was exhausted on their return, and there was no time to talk to others. The farmers had brought a better stove to their small home to help heat it, as the temperatures were dropping.

Mennonites in Ontario had their own recipes to make alcohol, and soon, Anna was making potato vodka and hiding it from her husband. They also had access to stores that sold alcohol, which opened up another avenue for those who now required it to get through their days. During the days, when the voices were loud, she was hungry, and she could do no more for the kids without screaming, she had a drink. It calmed the voices enough that they were nice to her and not so very judgemental.

George and Anna would make the journey back to Mexico after their work visa had expired in Ontario.George had more money in his pocket then he ever had in Mexico. He knew that with hard work and a better mastery of the language and customs he could fit in here and find a way to raise his children and prosper. He could see other Mennonite immigrants using their skills from "home" to make a living and this gave him hope that he could also make a good life in Canada. He would work hard in Mexico and save his money to come back again and he had connections this time that would help him get the work he wanted and his children would have enough to eat and a decent home. . George could feel the possibilities in Canada. He was going to learn English and get ahead. Come 1967, he would sign up again with the migrant workers to return to Ontario.

CHAPTER THIRTEEN:
CANADIAN BABIES

1967

Anna was heavily into the transition stage of labour and pushing, but this time in a hospital. She was having a Canadian baby. The labour was easier this time, and her panic wasn't as bad as it could get during birth, but in the hospital, everyone watched her, and too many people were looking at her private parts. She worried that these people might judge her.

When Anna arrived by car to the hospital, she had to change out of her dress. They gave her a cotton dress that was wide open in the back and didn't cover her bulging abdomen well. She didn't have underpants or a brassiere on, as she hadn't been able to sew since she'd arrived in Canada. Anna would have had the baby at home, but there wasn't enough room with the four other children in the bed, and her sisters weren't close by. Many of them were still in Mexico, making plans to come to Ontario. Others were in the Leamington area, working in the vegetable fields. She was alone for the first time for a birth.

Anna pushed and pushed as people watched her, and she tried not to yell out like the other times. She bit her lip until it bled and dug her fingernails into the mattress on the stretcher, trying to keep emotions under control. She had learned from her other labours that suffering to give birth was a gift from God and she need not share her pain with others. It was hers to bear. Still, the voices in her head were so loud during this.

You don't even deserve another baby. You're not a good mother.

CHAPTER THIRTEEN: CANADIAN BABIES

She shook her head side to side to keep the noise down and pushed again. It seemed to work.

She had learned to keep her voices to herself in Ontario. Even her family had a hard time understanding what she was saying when she described them or told them what the voices said to her. She would silence the voices inside her head by yelling, "Shut up!"

Each labour was hard, but today, she had a baby boy, and that always made George happy. He was their first son born in Canada. What a gift. Life was getting easier, and this boy would be the start of a good life in Canada. He looked just like his father, fair-skinned and blue-eyed. He was a blessing again. She could understand only a few words from the nurses and doctor as they delivered the placenta and moved her onto another bed to be wheeled to her room.

George was in the waiting room. He had been working when Anna went into labour, and she had the neighbour call the greenhouse to get the message to him. Then, the neighbour had brought her to the hospital. Anna didn't know many English words, but just looking at her panting was enough to make the neighbour understand what she needed. Gertruda had been left at home to care for the other children as they pulled out of the lane to go to the hospital. After seeing his son, George later picked up Gertruda and the children with her Gerhard's work truck and took them Gerhard and Margarets home.

Anna kept trying to get things right, act right, talk right, but each time she had a baby, she panicked about the additional work and the state of the house. Yet God would not give her a baby if she wasn't worthy. She had to make the best of it.

Anna held her son and looked into his blue eyes. Worry was heavier than joy in her chest that day as she stressed about his life and how he would turn out. She got up and started to get dressed. She knew they didn't have health insurance in Ontario, and she would have to pay if she stayed. She stood up to take off the thin gown, but blood gushed onto the floor. She didn't have underwear, and the nurse was frantically trying to find her clothing. The nurse shook her head, threw a towel on the floor, and sat Anna on the side of the bed. She got a basin and warm water and started washing Anna's thighs and calves and feet, covered in blood. Anna enjoyed having someone care about her and look after her for a change. The nurse found her some mesh underwear and put heavy pads inside. She motioned that she had extra pads for Anna to take home and laid them next to her clothing. She looked into Anna's eyes, and Anna could see her reflection in the nurse. She wasn't the person she thought she was. She wasn't her mutti or sisters. She was weak and alone. The reflection judged her just as the voices did, and she dropped her eyes to the floor.

Anna said "home," and the nurse nodded. The nurses were familiar with the Mennonites in the area. They all left after delivery instead of staying. Anna got dressed and pulled the apron over her large belly. The nurses had the baby wrapped up when Anna and George came into the room. George looked at his son and smiled. Another boy to carry on the name. George helped Anna get the baby into a blanket. Despite the nurse's concern, Anna felt that it had to get easier now. The nurse helped Anna to the wheelchair, and she held the baby on her lap. She was already exhausted and knew what the next few days would be like. At least with this baby, she would have enough milk to feed him. It had been a few years since she'd had enough milk to nurse regularly.

The nurse looked at that and asked, "Name? What are you naming your son?"

George said, "Peter," and they left the hospital.

Anna was happy to be home and needed to rest. This time, there were no neighbour girls to help or a sister to stop in with a meal. She was on her own, and Gertruda would have to be her helper. She was seven now, so she was getting strong enough to do chores around the house. George dropped Anna off and went back to work.

Anna's sister-in-law Margaret came over to help with supper and the other children. Anna lay with Peter in bed and fell asleep. The next thing she remembered was Margaret waking her up to nurse the baby, who was crying. Anna had not prepared any diapers or food for the baby, and Margaret was angry about this. She was ripping sheets and clothing to make temporary diapers until she could bring some from her house. There was no food in the cupboard to make a meal for the children, and she had to make boiled oatmeal to fill their stomachs. Margaret was better organized and worked quickly to clean the house. Diaper rags were stacked for the newborn, and the other children were excited to meet their new brother. It was a one-bedroom house they were renting, so Anna was able to get the bed. The children all slept on the floor around the living room and kitchen to have enough space. It was April and finally warmer, so they

CHAPTER THIRTEEN: CANADIAN BABIES

needed fewer blankets and clothes to cover the children and keep them warm. Anna was too tired to focus on the other children. She slept and slept.

In her head, she was repeating, *I'm just so tired. I'm tired of babies, meals, and this life of struggle.* Exhaustion from birth had caught up with Anna, and she would drift to sleep, wanting things like, *I wish I looked like the other mothers. I wish I had my mutti here to help me. I wish the voices would stop long enough so I could clear my head and get back to my job as a mother.* She knew it was a sin to wish for other things instead of being grateful for what God had provided, but she couldn't help it.

The kids ran and screamed in the yard, playing. They could make games out of anything, but mostly, they played hide-and-seek and bull and bullfighter, a game in Mexico the natives had taught them. They had an old blanket they used for the game, and they would run at the blanket headfirst to see if they could touch it before it was moved. George Jr. and Jake loved this game and would trick the smaller kids. One day, they held the blanket as little Maria ran with her head down to touch it. They held it in front of a tree, and when they pulled the blanket away, she ran straight into the tree and knocked herself out. She lay on the ground, unresponsive. The boys looked at each other and ran. Gertruda was helping Aunt Margaret hang clothes on the line and didn't notice her lying there. Margaret had brought over her own children to help Anna with the cleaning and meals. When Maria regained consciousness, she got up and touched her sore, broken nose. There was no one to hear her tears, so she held them in.

Since Anna and George had moved to Port Burwell, the county had been sending school superintendents to visit regularly. They couldn't understand what the officials were saying and relied on others to translate for them. The superintendents weren't very strict with them, as many Mennonites were moving in to the community and kept their children at home to work or be homeschooled. Gertruda, George Jr., and Jake were all school-age and sometimes tried to get on the bus and go to school. It was hard to understand the expectations of the schools, fit in at school with very little spoken or written English with George working, Anna in bed, and no food for lunches or clothing to wear. The bus went by their door, and if everything lined up, they got on it. Gertruda had shown signs of being a slow learner at a young age, unable to read or count money. In Mexico, reading was taught through the German

Bible—there was no English—so Jake and George Jr. had learned to read a bit from that.

In Ontario, George could get a contract for children over six to work; he wanted to get his children out and working to help them succeed in Ontario. He would bring Gertruda and Jacob with him to the cucumber greenhouses for the day, and they would make enough money to get groceries.

Since coming to Canada, going to church had not been part of their regular routine. Both Anna's and George's parents were Old Colony Mennonites, the most conservative of all the groups. In Mexico, their parents were expected to follow the word of the leaders and not submit to electricity or tractors with rubber tires. If they decided to be more progressive, they would be shunned, and many feared this, as it would have left them alone, unable to talk with families or friends. The struggles of other Mennonite families that they had met as migrant workers were the same as theirs. This helped Anna and George try and stay true to their faith and not fall to the temptations of electricity and progress. They could see area farmers using tractors and combines to plant and harvest their crops and the speed that they were able to work with only a few men. T The stress of staying true to values and faith was being tested against the advancement and prosperity in Mexico as well. George had heard from other families that many people had broken away from certain campos and were working with motorized machinery to produce better farms, healthier livestock and less focus on the words of the bible in their everyday life. This was a very conflicting time for them not knowing how to live without a colony but also knowing that if they took a risk they could have a life like their Ontario neighbours.

When Mennonites came to Ontario, churches were formed, but their power to determine how you lived, your transportation, and methods of dressing was diminishing as the families tried to find work and a way to be part of their new communities. Living in individual families with people of the world exposed them to more pressure to fit in. Never had any Mennonites in George's and Anna's families been immersed so independently into a culture that wasn't their own; many of George's brothers were still in Mexico, and only one of Anna's brothers, Gerhard, was in Ontario. They had never been allowed to think or plan on their own without the influence of their pastors and elders weighing on their decision.

CHAPTER THIRTEEN: CANADIAN BABIES

In Ontario, it was hard to try and fit in with the locals while not being seen as a failure in the eyes of God. Going to church was a place where everyone would judge them, and at the same time, they would see how successful others were with farming and their homes. It made George very angry. He was a strong, smart man, and he deserved the same as any other Mennonite. It wasn't easy because some Mennonites made money off his labour. They found him jobs because they could speak English and not him, but then they took part of his pay. He had to learn English faster to survive.

Anna wasn't welcome at church because of her temper and thoughts, which she was unable to hide as she had as a young woman in Mexico. It could have been because her family was no longer sitting with her in church to help her check in on the appropriateness of her actions, or it could have been that she felt God would love her no matter what she did. She would see other women looking at her, and she felt that they were judging her clothing, hair, and behaviour. She thought they were after her husband and perfect children at first. She felt more superior than the other women because of her direct communication with God through the voices in her head. When she had doubts about her specialness, the voices were there to boost her up. When they weren't there, they left an open space in her heart where she was alone and no longer special. The voices were both her friend and foe. Sometimes, they even made her hate her husband and children and yearn for the attention of other men in town.

On this day, Anna's new son, Peter, was almost a month old, and George was out of the house, working at the greenhouses with Gertruda, George Jr., and Jacob. Margaret had come over to her home and brought some food for the children: bread, meat, and hardened fat to act as butter. She hadn't even tried to wake up Anna. Margaret had watched her as she slept. *What would ever become of her?* she thought. *She needs to get up and look after these kids.*

But Anna was special. She just couldn't do things like other Mennonite women, and she was okay with that. She didn't want judgement from Margaret. When she woke that day, her entire body was heavy. She reached for Peter and took him to her breast to feed him as she rubbed the sleep out of her eyes. She was still sore from childbirth and repositioned herself on the edge of the wooden chair. They only had two chairs, so it was a challenge to get one with all of the children wanting to take turns using it. As Peter finished nursing, she put him into his basket, went under the kitchen sink, and found her bottle. She was always able to get isopropyl alcohol from local neighbours, as she told them it was for cleaning a wound. This allowed her even without transportation to still get it, drink it and feel calm again. It soothed the voices and made them less judgmental of her actions.

When George came home from work, he tossed a bag of bread and oatmeal onto the counter and looked at Anna. He had been able to buy the seconds of cucumbers and peppers from the greenhouse. "What's for dinner? Have you fed the kids yet?"

"I'm too tired. You bring home any flour or meat?"

George smashed his hand on the top of the table. "I work all day and you do nothing!" He picked up the bread on the counter and started to cut it up as each child stood in line for their share. They had a bit of leftover fat drippings from sausages in a tin that Margaret had dropped off earlier, and he spread this on the bread in place of butter. Anna put out her hand for her portion and got a crust. George took his bread outside, and most of the children followed. The house was so small that there wasn't enough room for all of them to stand and eat, and there certainly weren't enough chairs. Anna was famished. She couldn't remember when she last ate. She gobbled up the bread crust and looked at her children walking out of the door. *They all came from me*, she thought. *George might be the one angry, and they might follow him, but I'm here with all the children all day. They are all from me.* She smiled a bit as she watched them eat their bread and wander away.

Evening was upon them, and they all were getting tired. Anna settled into the bed with George. The rest of the children found a blanket and lay on the floor in rows like corn in a field. They all turned the same way to make enough room for everyone on the floor, and it was finally quiet.

CHAPTER FOURTEEN:
FAILING TO THRIVE IN ONTARIO

1967

The sun had risen in Vienna, Ontario, and the Peters children were awake and running around outdoors. With no shoes and barely clothing on, they were laughing, but they were also hungry. They came into the house to ask Anna for food. "There's no food here," said Anna. "Go to the neighbour to see if they have something to give us."

George Jr. and Jake smiled and gladly went out the door. They loved these adventures. They knocked on the neighbour's door and stood, waiting. Their pants were too short, as they had now outgrown them. They also had no shoes that would fit, so they were barefoot with dirty, uncombed hair but still with smiles on their faces. When the door opened, Jacob spoke. "Hello. Do you have any food that we can have?" They had been learning English as much as they could on the streets in Vienna and from other neighbours. They had to speak for their mom when they were out, but now, their dad was also learning the language at work and teaching them.

The neighbour looked at the boys, and her heart hurt. She said, "Wait here." She put together a package of bread, butter, lunch meat, and some fruit and handed it to the boys. "Do you not have any food at your house?" They both shook their heads. "Are you getting some help from the church?" The

CHAPTER FOURTEEN: FAILING TO THRIVE IN ONTARIO

brothers shrugged. They took the food with big smiles and ran home. Mom would be so happy now. The neighbour picked up the phone and called the Children's Aid Society (CAS).

At the house, the boys shared their food with everyone, and there was laughter as they sat together to eat. They buttered the bread and ate the meat, and that morning, their bellies were full. A few hours later, a police car came to the house. They knocked heavily on the door, and Gertruda answered it. She looked shyly at the officers and the woman with them.

"Are your parents home?"

Gertruda nodded.

"Can we come in?"

Gertruda stepped aside to let them in.

They walked into the two-room home with its two chairs and one bed to find all the children seated on the floor, playing. Anna was asleep in bed in the other room, and Maria was rocking the new baby. They walked around the small space and looked into the cupboard. It held a few chipped plates and big bags of oatmeal and puffed wheat cereal. All the food George Jr. and Jacob had collected in the morning was eaten, and the children were content.

Then, the officers gently shook Anna to wake her. She was very sleepy and smelled heavily of alcohol. She stirred and was startled to see strangers in the house. They tried to calm her, but she started yelling. It startled the kids, and they panicked and ran outside.

This time, there was only a warning to care for her children or they would be taken away. The social worker would check in on them and arrange some community resources. Anna nodded and looked at the ground. Policia in Mexico often came and took people away, and then they were never seen again. She swallowed hard as they spoke to her, understanding only a few of the words.

In the meantime, the bill had come from the hospital, showing the money they owed from Peter's birth. It was more than they could ever pay, and George worried about it. He showed it to others at work, and they said that the government would come after him for the money, so he had to pay it. He decided, as their summer of working the fields ended, that they would go back to Mexico and start work there. The bill could be left behind in Canada. They had made some money over the summer, totaling around $2,000. This would be enough to buy gas for the car and put a down payment on a farm in Mexico. In addition, his house wasn't insulated for the winter that was quickly approaching, so they didn't have any choice but to head back to Mexico and see if they could make a home there for now. Although it was dependent on the crops on Mexico, he still wanted to return to Ontario again for more money. He had learned to like the people, and his children were adjusting well to the English language. He also liked the idea of finally having some money in his pocket to take home.

It is now September and they had been working in Ontario since March,. They were now heading back to Mexico with much more money in their pockets, a better mastery of English, and an understanding of what life could be like if they lived in Ontario permanently. George loaded the children and Anna into the car after saying goodbye to Gerhard and Margaret, who were now seeking to stay permanently in Ontario. Gerhard had a nursery job, and he was able to have his children also work with him to earn extra money. His relationship with the newly established Old Colony church was also improving, and he was taking on more leadership roles. Margaret had packed a large lunch for George, Anna, and the children to help them get to Mexico.

It took them twelve days to get home to Cuauhtémoc, Mexico. The journey was long, with all the kids sleeping in the car and across the belongings, which were spread out on the back seat and floor. They had sold everything to go to Ontario, and along the way, they realized they would be starting over again in the next few months. But George knew that he could get a job working for other farmers or the cheese factory, and Anna would have the support of her siblings to raise the children. Warm thoughts of belonging and feeling the Mexican sun on their faces helped them manage the long journey.

CHAPTER FIFTEEN:
BACK TO MEXICO

1967

Anna and George crossed over the Mexican border with a sigh of relief. Their trip through the USA had gone fairly well, and they had enough gas left to get them to the campo. They'd left their old house behind before going to Ontario but knew they could stay with Anna's brother Heinrich while they found work and set up another home. He had six children of his own, so five more would be a challenge, but his wife, Anne, welcomed Anna and her family into their home and did her best to get everyone settled. The children were happy to play with their cousins and took to running outside.

Anna was exhausted. Her body felt heavy, and she was physically and mentally fatigued. The trip had made the voices in her head loud and forceful. They cast doubt on her worthiness as a wife, mother, and daughter. As she tried to unpack the car, she had to sit and reflect.

You're not good enough. You're not a good wife or mother.

These words kept repeating in her mind. Anne moved around her in a whirl, unpacking the clothing as George went to the barns to see his brother-in-law and set up some work.

The Old Colony church elders and pastor didn't welcome those that returned from Canada and referred to them as Kanadiars. They knew that they had been exposed to a life of sin and envy and didn't want them bringing new ideas to their congregations and communities. Many elders steered the

CHAPTER FIFTEEN: BACK TO MEXICO

returning families away from the community, but Anne and Heinrich did their best to defend and support George and Anna. The elders would be watching them to see how well they integrated into the colony and if they would be able to follow the old ways.

On their first evening in Mexico, Henrich brought up what he had heard from his brother Gerhard in Ontario about their time working there. "I know that you were having a hard time keeping Anna in line and not running around on you in Canada. I don't want that sort of thing here. She'll have to be a good Christian woman and look after the house and kids."

George was surprised and embarrassed that Heinrich knew. "You don't need to tell me how to manage my wife. She just needed to get away from Canada for a while. We'll make money here and get ahead."

George soon learned that there was no work on farms in the area owned by Mennonites. They had progressed while he had been in Canada. Some had good fields of crops, bought more cattle, and hired other Mennonites to work for them. Irrigation had been implemented in the fields of progressive Mennonites in other campos, and big farm tractors were doing the work that took weeks with horse and plow. But the Manitoba colony had not made those changes.

He was also discouraged at how far behind he was financially from others he knew. His brothers Johan and Wilhelm were also working for other farmers. In the evenings, George would go and visit them, but he didn't feel that he fit in there. As Mennonite families became more progressive in their farming and machinery, the leaders of the Old Colony church had excommunicated many of them.

Anne was busy preparing for her and Heinrich's own move to Ontario, but having extra bodies in the house was making it hard. They had to sell all their things to make the move while they had the additional burden of five children whose mother wasn't caring for them. Anna wasn't able to do her part in the house, not helping with the meals or caring for her own children. She spent many days lying in bed instead. She could feel the pressure to be a better wife, to fit in, and it overwhelmed her. This and a lack of sleep was making her depression harder to manage. She knew she needed a drink.

One night, she wandered away from the house in hopes of finding a hidden stash of homemade booze in a barn or even a Mexican with some mezcal she could barter for. She started out on foot as Anne was getting dinner organized for the children and didn't think she would be missed. She made it to a farm several miles away and was able to find a barn where men weren't working. She knew most men kept a stash of alcohol in the barns. She asked one young man walking by if he would share his stash, and he smiled and led her to his bottle. He watched her drink in amazement, as most women weren't open about this type of behaviour. He looked at her dark hair and wild eyes as she started to relax and sing before leaving her in the barn to finish his chores.

Anna sat inside and listened to the wind whistle through the boards. It was one of the first barns the community had built after coming from Manitoba. It was made of wood, and many boards had fallen off. It was hard to find replacements in the desert community. She felt the warm breeze turn cooler as she sat on the hay in her clothing from Ontario. They hadn't been able to keep up their conservative dress when they lived there, as she had no way to sew or care properly for her things. Now, she wore a floral dress without the traditional apron and pleating. She also had gotten away from wearing scarves over her hair when in Ontario, so she stood out when she was out and about on her own here in Mexico. It was warm weather, so ankle socks had to be okay.

She let the light of the moon soak into her as she thought about the last six months in Ontario. She had felt so alone and lost, lacking all direction and companionship. Her husband had left her behind as he'd found his way, working and meeting others. She, on the other hand, had no church and no women to talk with. She had never really fit in in Mexico because of her voices and her inability to read. She was known for having a short temper, and often, she would say things out loud that signalled she had an opinion on something women weren't expected to have, or say something that should have been saved for their women's quilting groups. When she moved to Ontario, she was again physically isolated from other Mennonite women, but also judged by the women of Ontario on how she dressed herself and her children. The only people she felt accepted and wanted by were the men she met around the farming town. They liked spending time with her. Even though she knew very little English, she knew how to please a man sexually, and that meant she had access to alcohol and company in payment.

She took a last long drink from the bottle and set it down as the sun faded behind the mountains. She could hear voices from outside, and then men

CHAPTER FIFTEEN: BACK TO MEXICO

approaching. As they came closer with lanterns, she could see it was her older brother Heinrich and her husband coming in.

George saw her first sitting on a bench outside of the barn as she finished the last bit of liquid in her bottle. "Get up from there! What are you doing?!" he yelled at her. The young man had led Anna to the barn and gone to find someone that knew her. Heinrich picked Anna up under her arm and stood her up, but she wasn't steady on her feet. She wanted to just lay in the barn and not leave. George and Heinrich guided her back down the road, staggering to the to the house. When they arrived, the children were all sitting outside at the wooden table. They had just had some *sup* for supper and were preparing for bed. The squeals of the children chasing chickens and running after each other drowned out Henrich and George telling Anne how they'd found Anna.

Anne shook her head and talked about how little Anna was doing to help with the kids. She thought it was a bad idea for George and Anna's family to be there while their own family had received their papers to go to Ontario and were getting ready to start a new life there. The fields had dried up, and the Mexicans were patrolling the roads, looking to take back their land. Tensions were growing in the campos, and Anne and Heinrich wanted to go now.

Anna sat quietly on a bench, feeling the effects of drink as she listened to the children and watched the sun set. George came over to her and said she should go to bed. They needed to leave the next day and would have an early morning. They had outstayed their welcome. Anna listened, anger building within her. Her own family couldn't turn her away. She started yelling at George, talking about how lonely she was and how much she missed the land and her family. She couldn't look after her children. It was all too much. She just wanted to have a break. All the adults were yelling, and it felt like no one was listening.

Gertruda had been listening to the conversation. She knew what her mother looked like when she drank too much, and it made her afraid. Gertruda had started talking to herself more, and in her head, there were voices who answered her. When she felt lonely or left out, she could talk to them. She shared this information with her mutti, but only privately; Anna never told her that she had the same voices. She never liked it when her parents would fight, even though she was used to it, because usually, one or both of them would leave. Their time in Ontario, with her mother in bed all the time and her father working, had led to many fights.

Gertruda listened to them fight and knew their family wasn't wanted in Mexico. Walking in circles in the yard just as she had seen her mutti do many times helped her formulate a plan. She saw that the fire was still burning outside in the cooking fire pit and got a stick to poke at it. The flames enveloped her stick and started to burn the wood. She took the stick and waved it in the air, watching the trail of light and smoke. Then, she brought her stick to the side of the house and touched the thatching on the roof. She watched as the flames sparked and took hold of the dried grass, then descend the walls of the house. She was surprised at how fast it moved at the edges of the roof and across it. Her first feelings were happiness, even joy, at watching the fire take over the thatch on the adobe home. The fire was justified because her cousins weren't treating her family well, and this finally might get her parents' attention enough to stop yelling. But the flames were growing too quickly due to the dry grasses, and she started to panic, running away so no one would know it was her who had started it.

The other children were in the house and could smell the smoke and see the flames. They ran outside, yelling, and that was when George, Heinrich, Anne, and Anna saw it. It travelled fast, and with the drought and low water levels in the well, they couldn't fetch enough water to douse the flames. Other neighbours saw the fire and came by horse and buggy, but it was no use.

Everyone stood and watched Anne and Heinrich's home and belongings burn as roof joists fell into the house—everyone except Gertruda. It took a while until others noticed she was missing. They feared she was in the house and called her name. Finally, she emerged from the desert night, and when they saw her, they instantly knew why she was hiding. Blaming, shaming, and despair surrounded all of them as they walked down the road to sleep in their neighbour's barn. There was nothing for Heinrich and Anne to take to Ontario now. There was no house to share with George and Anna. All was lost.

In the morning, George tried to reach out to other Mennonite farmers who might need a hired hand and have a place to rent for his family. Anne and Anna swept a section of the barn, preparing to make a temporary home there. Anna felt horrible about the fact that Gertruda had burned the house down, but she also felt relief. She wouldn't have to make the meals and care for the children so soon. There was nothing to start with, no expectations. She had freedom. The other family members, and cousins were very verbally abusive to Gertruda and

CHAPTER FIFTEEN: BACK TO MEXICO

shamed her for ruining their home. The little girl sat alone to one side and cried. It was hard for her to understand how this one act to distract herself from her parents fighting would change all their lives.

A week had passed, and many were turning their backs on George in his search for work. His Canadian ways were showing in the way he dressed, his expectations, and his inability to manage his family. He wasn't wanted on many farms. He had learned to be more assertive, challenging, and competitive than he'd been before Canada.

With no jobs and a future that seemed bleak in the region of Chihuahua where he'd grown up, George decided to return to Ontario. His Mexican community had turned their backs on him for seeking a better life. Unless he tried to fit in and allowed the leaders to enforce their rules, which included excommunication, he couldn't work with them, let alone prosper. Many others had been excommunicated, and they had a hard time fitting in unless they left the colony to marry Mexicans or moved to other towns. He knew that he could work in Ontario and wanted to stand on his own feet. If this community wouldn't have him or his children, he would find another that would.

He still had Gerhard and Margaret in Ontario, and they could help out when they returned. He had a few items in his car, and they sold what they could. He worked for Mexicans in the fields and in the cheese factory for a few days to get enough money for fuel and food for the journey. He knew that if he stayed here, he would only work for other more prominent Mennonites instead of ever owning his own farm and home. Working in the cheese factory was a way to get a few dollars, but it put more money in the rich Mennonites pockets, and he felt no more prosperous than the Mexicans working in the watermelon fields. He wanted something better for his family and himself, and he knew that if he had any chance of doing this, it would be in Ontario. These thoughts of envy and wanting would never be accepted in Old Colony thinking. As George made his plans to return to Canada, he was growing further from his roots.

Anne was trying to make a home from the corner of the barn as she and Henrich decided on their next steps. They could see Anna falling into a deeper state of depression and becoming withdrawn. It was a familiar situation for George, but no one else had seen this side of her. They prayed and prayed that she would have the courage to be a good wife and raise her family. The elders of the colony had heard about Anna and the fire, and it was only a matter of time before Heinrich and Anne would be excommunicated for their affiliation with the Kanadiars.

Anna was still drinking when she could find alcohol and not caring for the children. They ran in the red dirt, playing, and Anna smiled as she watched them. She couldn't make any decisions about what to do. It was overwhelming, and no one could pull her out of the darkness, not yet.

By the time George had enough money saved, he knew he could go back to Ontario to work in the fields for the spring and then apply for permanent status to stay there. They lived in the barn until the money was earned, and the children all worked in the fields, helping get food and fuel for the journey home. It wasn't a hardship for the children, as all their cousins also worked in the fields picking watermelon. They would work from dawn until dusk. They would laugh and eat watermelon as they worked. The women would bring wood, their cast-iron pans, and ground corn to make tortillas in the fields to eat with the watermelon. Every day was the same, but there was joy and fun in working with so many children and watching the girls' straw hat ribbons blowing in the hot Mexican breezes.

Anna was restless while she waited to go back to Ontario. She was used to not having someone watch her every move. Back here in Mexico, whenever she sat down for a short time, Anne would tell her to get up and do the wash, mend clothing, or feed animals. To escape this never-ending watch, Anna would go for walks and found that there were more Mexicans driving around the campos than she remembered. When she was a young girl, the fear of Mexicans and what they could do to a young woman was driven into her head by all the women and the church. But now, she looked at these men longingly. She wanted to prove to herself that they would be attracted to her just like the men were in Ontario and that the women in the campo had irrational fears about them. She also wanted a drink and didn't have a way to get any, so the Mexicans would be the solution.

That afternoon, a car drove by filled with three Mexican men, and they stopped as she walked by. "Hey. Want to come for a ride?" they asked in broken English. Just as the Mennonites tried to learn Spanish, the Mexicans were learning English in this region of the country.

Anna turned to look at the men in the car. "Got any booze in there?" They held up a bottle of half-finished tequila and shook it in her direction. Anna's eyes lit up. "I'll take that, but I don't have any money."

CHAPTER FIFTEEN: BACK TO MEXICO

The men said, "Well, no money, then no booze."

"I can do things for you, and then you can give me the booze," Anna offered. As soon as she said it out loud, her inner God spoke.

You're very pretty, and you deserve to have fun too. What could it hurt?

Anna climbed into the back of the car with one of the men, and he started to slide his hand under her skirt. "I get a drink first," she said. They let her drink out of the bottle before she let them have sex with her. She didn't care about sex. She looked out the back window as the other man sat in the driver's seat. When he was finished, she asked for another drink, and they gave it to her. She did the same with the driver, and eventually, they had drank all the tequila. Just as Anna staggered out of the car, a horse and buggy went by. Her brother Heinrich was in the driver's seat.

He craned his neck to look and saw her getting out of the back seat. He stopped the buggy and yelled in Spanish. "Get away from her. Anna, get over here now." Anna was surprised to see her brother and walked toward him. She had to pull up her panties that were around her knees and stumbled while doing so. Since moving to Ontario, she had learned about underwear and was proud to wear them as a sign of progress. Henrich had to pull her up to get her into the buggy as she was short and also dizzy from the alcohol. "Get away from here, you Mexicans. Leave our women alone!"

The Mexicans laughed and spun red dirt in the air as they drove away. They threw the empty bottle of tequila out of the window as they went. Henrich was so angry and ashamed. He looked straight ahead and not at his sister. Anna knew that he was angry and that he would tell George, but she didn't care.

You deserve to have fun too. Those Mexicans like you. You're a good catch for them.

Her inner voice was filled with reassurance. Anna looked at Henrich and saw the tightness of his jaw and his steady, forward gaze. She reached out to touch his arm, and he slapped her away. There were times when he had raped her in the barn as a young girl before she was married, yet he treated her with shame now.

"You sit there and look for forgiveness. You're a whore, just like Gerhard and George said. You're shaming our family."

Tears welled up in Anna's eyes. Her whole life she had embarrassed someone. She knew she wasn't a good mother or a good wife. She knew that sometimes, the voices told her to do things that others didn't agree with, and it made her angry. Why would she have the voices if they weren't from God? Why would God tell her to do things she knew were wrong? Anna was confused.

The ride to her brother's house was quiet. The movement of the buggy made her nauseated, and she had to turn her head and hang over the side to vomit on the way. The alcohol was stronger than what she could make or buy in Ontario.

When Heinrich arrived at his house, he stepped down and grabbed Anna's arm to get her off the buggy. George was already home. Anna fell to the ground, and Henrich kicked red dirt onto her. George and Anne came out of the barn. "What's going on here?" George asked and then looked at Anna's eyes. They were glassed over and vacant. He knew that look. He had seen it many times himself.

George grabbed one arm and stood her up. Henrich added, "I saw her get out of a car of Mexicans with her underwear pulled down. They had their way with her, but she wasn't fighting." George was furious. He had been shamed by his wife in front of his brother and sister-in-law. "You need to get out of here. You're not welcome anymore," said Heinrich, looking at George.

Anne nodded in agreement. "I can't feed all your kids and mine and look after our home. Anna doesn't help. She runs off in the day, and I don't know what she's doing. Others are talking. I don't want her here ruining our good name. You should go back to Ontario. You're not the same as when you left."

George could feel the anger growing within him. He grabbed Anna's arm, steered her to the car, and put her in the back seat before yelling for the kids to come from the yard. They were playing and chasing chickens and throwing rocks. "Get in the car. It's time to go." The children were confused but listened to him. George Jr. and Jake climbed in the front seat while Maria, Peter, and Gertruda sat in the back with Anna, who was sound asleep.

Heinrich looked at George and shook his head. "You could just leave Anna here and forget about her. She's not a good wife. Let the Mexicans have her."

George looked at Henrich and said nothing.

He got some gas on the way from the campo and drove across the border into the USA. Everyone let Anna sleep because they appreciated the silence. They would giggle and play games while Peter slept, and they could feel the rumble of the road under the floor of the car. In one small hole in the floor, they looked out onto the road to the concrete zooming by or tossed out stones from

CHAPTER FIFTEEN: BACK TO MEXICO

the foot compartment. This time, George didn't need an escort; he could speak enough English, he had some money in his pocket, and he was leaving Mexico behind for good.

They drove for the first few hours in silence, with only a few pieces of bread to eat and a bottle of water. George stopped a few times for gas and would buy corn chips for everyone. He knew from the bag what they would taste like and split them among the children. After three to four hours, a hot car, and too many corn chips, the children started throwing up. Anna woke to the smell in the car and began to throw up too. George pulled the car over to a car wash and hosed out the inside. The vinyl seats and the kids' clothes were covered with vomit.

He looked at Anna as she was trying to clean the kids. She acted like she hated him, and he knew that he had failed to control her behavior and to help her be a good Christian woman. He had given up many years ago, and yet he knew he had to keep her at his side. No one else would put up with her behaviour, and he had promised himself to her in marriage. At thirty-one years old, he felt completely alone in the struggle. His wife couldn't do her job, he couldn't do his, and his kids were all looking at him, wanting food and clothes that he couldn't provide. He felt very hopeless in the Missouri car wash.

Loading everyone into the car, he said, "No more food until we get to Ontario—just what we have packed in the car."

The kids all lay on each other and curled up to sleep. Anna stayed in the back seat and also slept. She knew he was angry but feared what her life would be like in Ontario again. She had no friends and no work. She couldn't milk cows or raise chickens because there was no money for any of it. She felt despair and immense loneliness. Even her sisters wouldn't understand her. They wanted her to act like them, and she never could. She could be so happy and they would still tell her to be quiet and stop being so jumpy. She could be so sad and they would still tell her to get up and do her work. She rarely felt that she was coping well at all. Her thoughts ran away in her head. The voices were distracting, but there had to be a reason she was chosen to hear them. She had to be chosen by God as the link to the average person. It was hard, though, and she tried to tune out the voices when they became too judgemental and critical. She loved them when they built her up and gave her confidence. But in the end, she couldn't escape them and the damage they caused her and her family.

George stayed focused on the road, and as he drove, he began to feel more optimistic. He had high hopes for what this permanent life in Ontario would give him and his family. He knew a way to get ahead, and he was desperate to have his turn at wealth and prosperity. He saw many people in Mexico that he'd grown up with who had broken from the church to find a way to succeed and thrive. He knew that it was possible to live without the leadership of a pastor and elders now, and he felt that this was the only way that he could succeed in this modern world without Mennonites to support him. He needed to be just as inventive, to trust his gut, and to take advantage of opportunities. He looked across the seat to his sleeping children. He would give them a better life.

In the rearview mirror, he saw Anna sleeping with his other children. What would he do about her? He didn't know, but things had to get better. He didn't love her anymore. She had betrayed him, embarrassed him and his family, and he'd lost all respect for her. But he had to stand by her because he was married to her.

He drove day and night, crossed the Canadian border, and finally arrived at Gerhard and Margaret's home.

"What are you doing back here?" Gerhard asked. "You need to get a contract to work in the fields with a farmer, and you don't have that arranged yet."

George nodded. "Yes, I do. I did that from Mexico. I have work and so do the children, starting next week. We need to stay here until I can get the house arranged, and then we can start building our life again."

Gerhard shook his head in disapproval. "Henrich let us know what Anna was doing in Mexico. She can't be doing that here. You need to take better care of her," he said as George unpacked the car.

George was abrupt. "I do my best with her, but she's not right in the head, and she won't listen. She won't care for the kids, and she drinks too much and hides it all over the barns and house. There's rarely a time when she isn't drunk. I can't watch her and work too."

Anna was slow to get out of the back seat of the car. She had puffy eyes and looked dazed. She had slept most of the route back, eating only minimal corn chips and water. She walked past him, inside the house, and upstairs to lie on the floor and sleep. Margaret saw Anna go into the house and looked at the children. They were dirty and half dressed. Their clothes had been soiled from the long journey, with only a few weeks in Mexico before being turned away

CHAPTER FIFTEEN: BACK TO MEXICO

from the colony. There were no diapers for the trip, so the smells of urine and stool permeated the air.

Anna was sleeping when Margaret finished bathing the children upstairs and put them to bed on the floor with her own children. As Anna snored, lying on her back, Margaret noted the size of her stomach. Anna was pregnant again.

In the morning, George was up early. He had arranged a ride with Gerhard to get information about his work and buy some food with his leftover money. By now, Gerhard was the supervisor of the greenhouse workers. He had been working hard to get ahead and feed his family, and the company recognized him for this. They had given him a two-story home on the greenhouse site. He had learned English and was the interpreter for migrant workers, as well as the manager of the greenhouse.

George found out there was a house he could have for his family while he worked. He was excited to be out from under Gerhard's roof, as Gerhard was expecting him to work and care for Anna and the children. Margaret no longer wanted to teach Anna more skills on managing a home, as she slept most of the day. George went with Gerhard to the old schoolhouse they had arranged for him to rent. The roof was leaking, and the floorboards were broken in some areas. It had drop toilets in the house and a water pump outside, but there was electricity and a stove. George walked around and looked at the possibilities and smiled. Gerhard said he could get some beds from the church women, including some bedding and blankets. George nodded. This could work out well for his family. It was bigger and better than the last house they'd lived in before going back to Mexico.

They drove back to Gerhard's, and he told the kids and Anna about the house. Gertruda, George Jr., Jake, and Maria were all old enough to work in the fields and greenhouse with him. They could get more money as a family. Hard work was the only way ahead, and George was ready to do it. Anna sat quietly while he described the dream. She had been so distracted with the drive home, sleeping, and the voices that she hadn't noticed the kicking of a new life within her stomach. George could tell by looking at Anna that she was with child again. He had mixed feelings about this; it added pressure to get everyone settled into a home.

Over the next few weeks, George and his family moved into the old former schoolhouse. The children loved it. It was big and had high ceilings. Next to the house was a forest. They weren't used to seeing a field of trees; in Mexico, trees were rare because they were hard to keep alive. They'd never seen so many trees together. There were trees and a farm next door with pigs that wandered in the fenced fields. It all seemed to be working out.

"I'm going to get work. I'm taking all the kids except Peter. I'll bring home groceries. There's a washbasin and water outside to heat for the wash. We'll be back after six." Anna just looked at him as she sat on the side of bed.

Among the collected items was a wringer washing machine. As Anna started to figure out how to use it, Margaret came in. She'd had her oldest son drive her over after she'd collected clothes from other Mennonite families, as well as bread, canned beans, and butter. Margaret couldn't stay, but she looked at Anna and the pile of dirty diapers.

"You need to soak those first before putting them in the washer." She showed Anna how the machine worked and nodded. "George and the kids are working and will be hungry when they get home. Try and be ready with their supper." Anna just nodded. How could she do the laundry and get dinner ready? She wasn't able to multitask that day. She worked for a short time but couldn't wring out the clothes before she had to sleep again. Peter was also sleeping.

It was growing dark outside when everyone came home. The noise of chatter filled the house, and everyone was tired but excited. Anna hadn't been up long enough to think of dinner, and George saw the washing machine filled with water and dirty diapers.

"Anna, what did you do today? You didn't even make us dinner."

Anna yelled back, "I can't do it alone. I don't feel well. I can't do it."

George listened carefully. "Gertruda and Maria can stay home to help you out here. Gertruda is nine now, and she can do the washing."

Anna nodded as she watched George cut bread and hand some to the kids. While he'd been working that day, he had heard of work in the tobacco-drying barns. He would take his oldest boys with him after the greenhouse and work there.

In the morning, George had a routine of bringing in a pail of water from the well, setting it on the counter, and having bread from the previous night before leaving. Anna would be in bed, and Gertruda and Maria would get up, clean Peter, and find their breakfast. Gertruda started the washing machine and put

CHAPTER FIFTEEN: BACK TO MEXICO

the clothes through the wringer. She found some rope to make a clothesline and was hanging out the clothing when a car pulled into the laneway.

A woman got out as Gertruda hung out her wash. "I'm Debbie from next door. Do you have everything you need? This is a pretty old house, and it must be hard to keep it clean." Gertruda said nothing to her. She didn't understand English very well. "We just live over there," she pointed across the road. "If you need anything, just come on over. Are you excited about school?" She handed Gertruda a wicker basket of eggs, bread, and meatloaf as a welcoming gift. Gertruda just nodded. Debbie drove off.

Gertruda was excited to bring the basket into the house. "Mom, Mom, look!" She woke her mother by yelling. Anna sat up and listened to the story from Gertruda. She looked at her and smiled. Gertruda was the spitting image of her. She too was gifted with the voices, and Anna knew they would always have each other for support. They understood each other.

"Can we go to school?" she asked.

Anna looked at Gertruda, knowing she would have a hard time learning, just like she did. "No. You stay at home and work. School won't be right for you."

Gertruda listened but hung her head. She wanted to go to school and try.

Anna ate from the basket as Maria and Gertruda made a snack for Peter. "I'm going into town for a bit." She stood, put on her shoes, and fixed a scarf around her dark hair before walking out.

Gertruda, Maria, and Peter stayed home. The laundry was hung out, and Gertruda swept the floors in the schoolhouse and sorted out the clothes that had been dropped off by the local church. Gertruda and Maria shared a bed, and Jake and George Jr. shared another. Peter had a crib, and Anna and George had their own bed. At each end of the building were doors marked Boys and Girls, and the same with the bathroom. The drop toilets were foul-smelling from previous years of use without cleaning or emptying them, and the doors were broken, but there were no other options. Old chalkboards lined the walls of the three rooms, and there were scraps of chalk left, which they could use to draw. None of them could write the alphabet or their names; it wasn't something they had the opportunity to learn yet.

Anna started the two-kilometer walk into town. She needed a drink and missed that from her life in Mexico. She knew that men would get her a bottle if she offered sex. Sex didn't mean anything to Anna. She knew how to pleasure a man and not get pregnant, so she would do that. God didn't approve of making a baby out of wedlock, but He said nothing about pleasure.

She met a man outside the bar. He was a dark-skinned farmworker. Anna had a few English words to use, but she hoped he might speak Spanish or Plautdietsch.

"Hello," she said to him. He turned to look at her. "I need booze, but I got no money. I can give you sex if you buy me a bottle."

He looked at her from top to bottom, noted her pregnant abdomen, and shook his head. "You should be taking it easy on drinking with that baby in there."

"That's no baby. I'm just fat. Come on." She moved closer to him. She was still a pretty woman. Her dark eyes and white skin were prominent behind her floral scarf.

He looked again. "Okay. What do you want to drink?"

"Tequila or whiskey."

He walked into the liquor store and came out with his bottle. He led her to his car and unzipped his pants. Anna bent to her knees and paid for her bottle with oral sex. She focused on how she would feel when she drank the bottle during this act. When she was done, she put her hand out for the bottle and smiled. She unscrewed the lid and took a big drink and walked home.

She lost her way, and it was almost dark when she got home. George was back from working, and Gertruda had tried to find enough for supper. Anna walked in, smelling of alcohol, and went to her bed. George looked at her state. He followed her to the bed, where she flopped down and was asleep almost right away. He nudged her and spoke. "Where have you been? What are you doing drinking?"

"Get away from me. Go to hell!" Anna screamed.

George stepped away and went to sit with the kids. Nothing was changing, and little did he know, it was only going to get worse.

CHAPTER SIXTEEN:
RETURN TO ONTARIO

1968

Anna was in the hospital, pushing and groaning until her baby was born. She delivered a boy. He was small, but he was breathing on his own. Anna had gone into labour while she was drunk, so the effects still lingered as the nurses cut the cord and wrapped the baby. They didn't let her see her son right away, and she was okay with that. Instead, she lay down to sleep. The baby was jaundiced and whisked away to an incubator for closer observation.

The doctor came into the room and tried to wake her. "Anna. Anna, we need to talk about your health." Anna moaned and looked at him through slitted eyes. "Your skin is yellow, and your liver isn't working right. We can't let you go home right now. You're very sick, and you might die if you don't stop drinking."

Anna looked at the skin on her hand. She hadn't noticed that her skin was turning yellow. She shrugged at the doctor's explanation and went back to sleep. They started an IV, giving her medicine and vitamins.

George was working when his son, John, was born. He received the message at the greenhouse to go to the hospital. He drove in his brother-in-law's truck and went to the obstetrical unit. He peered in the viewing window for the baby with the Peters name and found his baby, another boy. George smiled to himself and went to find Anna's room. They couldn't stay long in the hospital, as they weren't residents yet and couldn't get free healthcare. He saw the nurse at the desk, and she followed him into his wife's room.

CHAPTER SIXTEEN: RETURN TO ONTARIO

Anna was sleeping on the white sheets, and that was when he really noticed how yellow she was. The nurses asked George to wait until the doctor could come and speak to him. He nodded, went closer to Anna, and touched her arm to wake her. "Anna, are you okay? We have a new son, Anna." He could hear feet approaching and turned to see the doctor and nurse.

"Hello, Mr. Peters. Your wife has liver failure because of her alcoholism. If she doesn't stay in the hospital and get treatment, she will die. She needs help with her drinking."

George was surprised that Anna was drinking enough to cause such damage. He had known of other Mennonites who'd died from too much drinking, including Anna's father.

"We don't have any insurance. We can't afford to stay in the hospital."

The doctor insisted they shouldn't worry about that right away. They couldn't let Anna go home the way she was. But George knew he couldn't care for a new baby and work at the same time. He made it clear to them that he wasn't able to cope with this change, and the CAS was called. George went to hold his son in the nursery. He looked at him and called him John. He put him back down and then waited to meet with CAS and find a solution to his family problem. CAS took John with them the next day, and George left Anna, jaundiced, in her bed. He went home and told the children that Anna wouldn't be home right away and then went to work again.

It would take three months before Anna was well enough to come home. She went through delirium tremens, a form of severe alcohol withdrawal, while in the hospital and was weaned off the alcohol. Her liver damage was partially reversible; with abstinence, it could heal and function again. Anna's milk had dried up with her hospitalization, and so they used formula for baby John. After three months, she felt ready to come home. She had learned a lot of English while she was in the hospital but still hadn't told anyone about the voices in her head. Her mother had always made it clear that no one else would understand. The voices were loud and gave her much praise for how well she was doing and how admired she was by the doctor and nurses.

George and CAS coordinated her discharge home and care of John. In the meantime, George had started spending a few evenings a week after his late shift at the Vienna Hotel having a few drinks and getting to know more English and the local men. George had been going to the Vienna Hotel after his long work days in the fields and greenhouses and he overheard the owner commenting that he could use some extra help at the bar. George asked if he would consider hiring him, he admitted to having no skills and, basic English, but he was a reliable worker. He was hired on the spot and after a few short shifts he was hired with a regular schedule. He was feeling better about his life but was bringing in barely enough money for his rent and food. His car needed repairs, which he couldn't do on his own, but it was finally fixed with the help of a few men in the field that he met. He didn't own tools, but with the machinery always needing repairs, they helped him and told him what parts were needed to fix the car.

Since George worked every day and into the evenings, Gertruda and the children were taking care of themselves. They had the house ready for Anna and their new brother. John had been born in June and now, at the end of August, Anna was coming home with him.

School trustees had been around to let George know that his children should be going to school. He was conflicted about the idea. He needed the boys' help in the greenhouses, but they hadn't been able to learn any reading or math in Mexico, so he considered this opportunity important. He wanted to prepare them for success in Ontario.

Their residency papers had finally been approved, and they could stay in Canada. Both Anna and George's parents were Canadians, so it took less time than it would with other migrant workers. Soon, their health insurance would begin and help cover the medical bills. Life in Canada was getting better for all of them, and with Anna healthy and out of the hospital, maybe they would have a better home here.

First winter in Ontario, George and family

CHAPTER SEVENTEEN:
HOPE AND NEW BEGINNINGS

1971

George had been offered a new job as the bartender at the hotel he frequented, the Vienna Hotel. His wages and the tips were more money than he'd ever earned, and he admired the owners and respected them for trusting him with managing the cash till and helping with opening and closing the hotel. He was capable and knew how to follow the rules of serving, making sure there was no risk to the owners' business. He took pride in his ability to settle down the rowdy drunks simply by standing still beside them. His large frame and height discouraged any revelers and made sure that no one was hurt or that no furniture was broken.

He felt like he was part of a team with his coworkers by his side. He liked them all, and they understood and accepted him, a first for Canada. While working the bar in the evenings, he'd met an amazing woman. She often came with her friend Ellen to visit with the locals, hear the gossip, and meet the farmworkers who were helping for the season. She was known as Tootsie, although her real name was Irene. She had a smile that brightened a room, and she laughed at the silliest things. She also had a genuine interest in George and his family. She was divorced with children but knew that George was still married. His wife wasn't a big part of his life anymore, and he was working double shifts to provide a

CHAPTER SEVENTEEN: HOPE AND NEW BEGINNINGS

better home for his children. He often slept at the bar overnight because he was so exhausted that he couldn't deal with what was going on at home. George wasn't specific about his life, but Tootsie knew it was only a matter of time until he left his wife and would be able to look after his children properly.

Tootsie was a nurse at a local nursing home, kind, caring, and hardworking. She was raising her children on her own with the occasional help of an ex-husband in town whenever he remembered to send her money. She didn't feel guilty for going to the bar for a drink after her work shifts, housekeeping, and meal preparation for her children. Her friend lived close by and helped her out as much as she could to balance life as a single mother and still have time for herself.

As she started to get to know George, her family also got to know him. They discovered that he was kind and loved to laugh and joke around. This was part of what made Tootsie fall in love with him. George loved spending time with her and knew that he could share private details of his life and not be judged. They respected each other. He had seen strong women in the Mennonite colony get silenced, but he wanted to listen to Tootsie, and she respected him just as he did her. He liked to be able to talk to a woman and have her answer honestly without fearing disappointing from her husband, church women, or leaders or fearing discipline for her ideas. Tootsie said things as they were, and he approved of her honesty and hard work.

George made sure he regularly sent money home for food, but he had no idea how much money was used for food and how much for alcohol. Anna had started drinking again almost as soon as she came home from the hospital. The house was full with six children, and she never had any time for herself. She became used to delegating chores to Gertruda. Jacob and George Jr. were old enough to fetch water and help with the others. She never really bonded with John when he came home. He was constantly crying, hard to keep content, and she felt less confident in her abilities. She was getting tired of having babies and raising children. The responsibility was too much on her own.

The CAS social workers and school trustees checked in regularly to make sure Anna was sending the kids to school. The social workers would try to teach Anna skills and link her with community resources to help with her transition to life in Ontario, but Anna didn't understand them and didn't want to listen to outsiders about how to live her life. She hadn't developed any trust in the community members, as each time they came, they tried to take her children or tell her how to live in her own home. It wasn't often that all the children would be up and ready for school when the bus came to the end of the laneway. They had no alarm to wake them, food for their lunches, or clean clothes, so they stayed home. They would be teased at school for their poverty, and it made fitting in and learning English even more challenging. Gertruda was trying to do her mother's job, including laundry and cleaning the house. Maria would help as she could while trying to care for Peter and John.

Anna had dark days during her struggle with depression, and Gertruda and Maria performed skits for her, dancing and singing, to see if they could get her to smile. She would occasionally laugh out loud, and that relieved the burdens of everyday life in the schoolhouse. Gertruda was starting to hear more voices and began talking to them. Anna recognized what was going on and became jealous that she wasn't the only one God was speaking to. She punished Gertruda by giving her less food or hitting her for forgetting to do chores. She needed to make sure her daughter knew she wasn't as special as her mother was.

On a regular basis, Anna would walk to town or the nearby farm to get money for more booze or a ride to the liquor store. The farmer across the road would often be out with his pigs in the field and had been seen helping Anna into his truck for the trip to town. In exchange for a ride to town, Anna provided oral sex, and he often let her have some meat or eggs. When he wasn't around, she would find a migrant worker in town instead. *They all love me*, she thought. Her English was getting better, even with a heavy German accent. Most of the migrants spoke Spanish as well, so Anna could understand and converse with them in basic words. She had many clothes to choose from, donated by charities and other families. She could dress up in local clothing, not Mennonite wear, and men wouldn't see her any differently from other women. She was wearing bras and formal underwear, which Mennonite women weren't allowed to do because they demonstrated vanity. The garments were often too sexual or alluring to be accepted by the elders in the colony and the pastor. When she'd returned to Mexico the last time, she'd worn a brassiere, and her sister-in-law Anne had cut it off of her. It was proof of vanity and ties to the devil. Anna would never be accepted into the congregation if anyone knew she had succumbed.

CHAPTER SEVENTEEN: HOPE AND NEW BEGINNINGS

Back in Ontario, she still braided her hair and put a scarf over her head, as she didn't know anything else, but she was happier with the modern clothing. She was petite and had a cute figure despite her eight pregnancies. She enjoyed the attention of men and the feeling of being popular. Since George was rarely home, she'd started bringing men back to the old schoolhouse for sex. The voices in her head reinforced that what she was doing was okay. She knew that they wanted her to be loved and happy. With sex, she could gain attention in a way that she never could before. Men would wait to see her and want to spend time with her. She presumed George was also seeing other women, but they never talked about it. They rarely saw each other anymore. When she brought the men home, they would all come with a bottle of whiskey for her.

Gertruda and Maria would be in the same room, as they all shared a bedroom. The babies, Peter and John, would be in the crib together, and George Jr. and Jake would be out exploring in the woods beside the house. When the men came over, they looked at Gertruda and Maria with a keen interest. Anna noticed this, and it made her proud. Her eldest daughter looked just like her, and the younger one was blonde, fair, and blue-eyed. Gertruda was eleven now and Maria seven. The men started coming with two bottles of whiskey so they could also have time with one of the girls. Anna would start drinking her bottle, not caring what happened to her daughters. They would have to learn on their own, like she did, what men wanted and how to get what you needed too.

Gertruda and Maria shared a bed, and the men would come over and lie between them. Often, Maria would run off and hide under her brothers' crib or bed. Gertruda, on the other hand, didn't understand what was happening. Because she saw approval in her mother's smile, she let the men do what they needed to. Most of the men were migrant workers, and some were local men who had heard about the opportunities to be with young girls. They would often just rub her and ejaculate on her legs or clothing. Maria received the same treatment, but she fought more. The weight of the men combined with the smell of sweat, whiskey, and rough beard would make her panic, and she would start crying. Gertruda rarely cried, making her more appealing. Once the girls became more aware of the risks, there were times when they would run from the men. The men would trap them in the corner of the room and physically take them to the creaky steel twin bed to lay with them. Anna would be drinking or already drunk, and she would talk to herself or laugh alone in the room while she watched her daughters.

More and more men would be in the house when the kids came home from school. Anna hadn't prepared any food for the children, as she used any money she had to buy alcohol and take off with random men. Sometimes, Anna would be gone for several days; with no food or telephone, the children would try to survive by their own means. They would walk into town and beg for money for bread or go to the pig farmer in the hope that his wife had extra eggs or baking. During one long stretch, George came home to drop off money and found the children all about the house, dirty and hungry. He asked where Anna was, and no one knew. By this point, the neighbours had called CAS, and arrangements were being made for the children to be placed in foster care until Anna could be found and a parent would be able to care for them. George never saw that it was also his responsibility to ensure his children were being watched. He was raised expecting that was the woman's role where his role was to work. George went to Gerhard's home and asked if they knew where Anna was, but they didn't. Anna's sister Agatha had moved from Mexico and was in the Aylmer area with her own six children, but Anna wasn't there either.

The children were placed in separate homes. Some went to Mennonite families, and others didn't. George Jr. and Jake were kept together, then Gertruda and Maria, and then Peter and John. It wasn't really so bad. While they were in care, they had baths, three meals a day, and went to school each morning, and at school, they got to see each other again and catch up. Their lives had been defined by a lack of parenting, rules, or education, so this big change was a tough transition. They knew little of rules and reminders of routines and expectations. None of the older children had been to school consistently, so reading was a challenge. Gertruda couldn't read or write, and George Jr. and Jacob were doing their best to learn. The foster homes were unclear on how long they would be having all of the children as Anna and George needed to be deemed suitable parents. With the consistent meals and clean clothing, the children were putting on weight and looking less disheveled. They were sleeping in their own beds and feeling more secure in a stable home environment, but at the same time worried about their parents and when they would all be together again.

Anna returned from her latest drinking binge with a migrant worker to find her children gone. She lay down to sleep, not considering where they might

CHAPTER SEVENTEEN: HOPE AND NEW BEGINNINGS

be. She just knew she needed some rest. George finally caught her at home and pushed to know where she'd been. He finally told her the kids had been taken away.

"They're my kids. They can't take them away," she blurted.

George agreed that they needed to take better care of them and that Anna needed to stay home, use the money George provided for food, and do the chores around the house.

Anna just nodded. Her inner voices were very loud these past few days.

He has no business telling you how to live your life. You're just as popular as he is, and you deserve to have fun. Anna smiled. She knew the voices were right.

Margaret came over and helped Anna to clean the house, catch up on the piles of dirty clothing, and get some food in the fridge so the social workers could inspect the house and bring back the children. The next day after school, the social worker loaded up the children and brought them back home. They returned with mixed feelings. Each of them got to bring home their new clothes and books from school. Anna and George greeted them, and they all sat together for a meal. George went to work that evening for the night shift at the hotel, and Anna crawled into bed.

The next day, they got up alone, readied themselves for school, and walked down the lane to catch the bus. Peter and John were home alone with Anna, and she wasn't out of bed yet. She had entered another depressive phase. The kids learned to avoid her during these times and just live their lives. At school, they had made a few friends, and despite not having much education, they were all quick learners. Gertruda struggled the most and was prone to fighting, as she had trouble getting along with other girls her age. She didn't speak very much since she was shy and grew accustomed to staying silent so others wouldn't think she was slow. Gertruda didn't see a reason to embarrass herself.

When they got home from school, Anna, Peter, and John were gone. The children knew there was a bag of oatmeal and some powdered milk, so they made some dinner, played outside until dark, and put themselves to bed. Anna didn't come home, and they didn't seem to notice. They'd gotten used to looking after themselves.

That day, Anna had met Pierre, a Quebec worker in the tobacco fields. He had finished his contract and was celebrating when Anna saw him coming out of the liquor store. She smiled and offered companionship for the bottle he had.

He agreed. They only had to make one stop before they could start their fun-filled few days. She needed to get her two sons and drop them off at her sister Agatha's, and Pierre drove her where she needed to go.

"I need you to look after the boys for me. I'm going away for a little while," said Anna as she handed her sons to Agatha.

Agatha was confused. "Where's George? Where are the other kids? Where are you going, and who is this?"

Anna waved away her questions, with Pierre smiling in the doorway. Agatha had four of her own children at home that she could barely feed. Tears welled up in her eyes as she thought of Anna and the life she was leading. Agatha knew she couldn't care for these extra children and took the brave step to walk over to the neighbours' to call CAS.

At school, police cars were waiting outside again as Gertruda, George Jr., Jake, and Maria finished school. "You need to come with us again. You're staying with another family while we find your mother." This was embarrassing for all of them. It was hard enough making any friends or relationships at school when they would only attend on and off, and now, this made it seem like they were in trouble. They were split up again. Peter and John were collected from Agatha's house and put in foster care like the other children. At the hotel, George was notified that his wife was missing and that his children were back in foster care.

Anna would disappear almost weekly and leave the children alone. It was almost a relief when she was gone as other men would not be coming to the house at all hours of the day and night. At one point, George took the girls to Tootsie's house to get their hair washed. It was matted and hadn't been combed for days, and they had been going to school like that. When they were at Tootsie's home, they discovered that the girls' hair was too matted to be combed out, and they had to take the girls for haircuts. While they were out, George and Tootsie got them ice cream and new dresses. Maria was soaking up the kindness but knew how angry their mother would be about their hair. Mennonite women didn't cut their hair. She could feel an ache in her stomach from thinking about the yelling and not talking for days that would occur when Anna saw them.

George dropped the girls off at home, and Maria went to hide. She didn't want Anna to see her hair. Gertruda, on the other hand, walked in proudly to show her mother. "Look, Mom. We got new dresses and our hair cut."

CHAPTER SEVENTEEN: HOPE AND NEW BEGINNINGS

Anna opened her eyes as she lay in bed and saw that her beautiful daughter's hair had been cut. Her braids were gone. Gertruda twirled around to show her clean new dress, and Anna sat on the side of the bed.

She reached out and slapped Gertruda across the face. "You look like a whore. You are no daughter of mine," she yelled. "Where is Maria?"

Gertruda pointed to the next room, and Anna went in, throwing the door back. Behind the door stood Maria with her shoulder-length hair. Anna grabbed her by the hair and pulled her into the room. She feverishly ripped the dresses off Maria and Gertruda before going to the kitchen to set them on fire, burning the dresses in the front yard of the house. Anna then went back inside while Gertruda and Maria stood naked, watching their lovely purple plaid dresses with purple satin ribbons burn. They both knew better than to cry. In the end, they walked into the house, found some pajamas to wear, and crawled into bed together.

Anna's drinking would cause liver failure once more, leading her to hospitalization, and the children would again do their best to cope in multiple foster homes. Agatha tried to reach out to Anna again to see if she could teach her about mothering, but Anna wanted no advice from her sister.

In the meantime, George was trying to build up his bank account enough to take the children away from Anna. He was saving money to rent a house big enough for everyone, including Tootsie and her family. He had to do something but couldn't be at home and work extra hours to get enough money. His relationship with Tootsie was growing. They were becoming intimate partners in trying to save his children and care for them properly.

Gerhard had heard that George had a girlfriend and blamed the family troubles on him instead of his own sister for running off. He refused to acknowledge that Anna was an alcoholic, prostituting herself and her daughters to get the drink she needed. He knew his sister had had mental health problems her whole life and was convinced that if George was home more and kept her in line, she would be a good mother and wife. But George had given up on trying to change her and was instead planning a life without her, one with just his children and Tootsie.

As the voices grew louder in Anna's head, she would bring more and more men home. Anna allowed them to have her and her daughters, and the older boys stayed out of the house when they were there. Some of the encounters would end with the men slapping Anna or pushing her out of the way to get to the daughters. She was often bruised, but as long as she had a drink, she tolerated the abuse.

"Girls, come in the house with me for now," she yelled to them in the yard one day. She took Gertruda's hand, and she willingly walked with her mother. Gertruda adored Anna, who always said they looked alike, and she liked being special that way. She also knew that hearing voices was something she shared with her mother. When school was hard and learning to read seemed impossible, she would take comfort in the fact that she had the voices to guide her. Maria ran across the yard when she was called and followed behind her sister. She felt the hand of the strange man on her back, pushing her toward the house. She wasn't convinced that he was a good man or that he should be trusted. She didn't like the feeling she was getting as he smiled down on her.

As they entered the house, Anna led the girls to the bedroom. "Gertruda lay on the bed there and let Jim see you. He wants to get to know you." Jim looked at Anna and nodded. She said to him, "It's $20 or a bottle of whiskey to be with my girl. No sex, just touching. You don't violate her." Jim handed her the money and went to the bed to grin at Gertruda. Maria watched as he approached her sister, and fear rose within her. This was wrong. This wasn't how it should be. Anna watched as he pulled up her dress and put his hand in her panties. Anna told her daughter, "It's okay. You'll like him, Gertruda. He really likes you." She smiled at Gertruda. She trusted her mother, and so she let him lie in the bed with her. Anna started drinking in the bed next to them.

When he was done with Gertruda and had masturbated on the bedding, he looked toward Maria. "The pretty blonde is more to my taste," he said. "I'll give you $40 for her." Anna's eyes lit up. She pushed Maria to the bed and grabbed Gertruda by the arm to get her off it. She forced Maria to lay down even though she was scared. Jim put the weight of his arm across her chest and lifted her skirt. She started to cry and looked at the old bed frame to focus her attention on other things as he smelled her hair and touched her face. It had five posts. 4+1=5. 3+2=5. She counted in her mind as she cried and tried not to think of this man on her. She just wanted to learn and go to school. She started to scream, and Anna yelled at her to shut up. Jim realized this wasn't what he'd hoped for and stood up beside the bed. Anna took him to her bed. Gertruda

CHAPTER SEVENTEEN: HOPE AND NEW BEGINNINGS

crawled back on the bed with Maria and they lay quietly, sobbing as they heard their mother and Jim in the next bed.

Outside the old schoolhouse windows, George Jr. and Jake watched. Maria could see them peering in, but none of them knew what to do to help. They all knew this was wrong.

Jim paid Anna, and then she said, "Will you take me to the liquor store?"

He shook his head no.

"Come on. Take me to the liquor store. The fun doesn't have to end here."

He hit her across the face. "You stupid bitch. I'm not taking you anywhere."

Anna hit him back, and he hit her even harder, Knocking her onto the floor. George Jr. and Jake ran to the neighbours for help. The girls crawled into the crib with Peter and John, and they huddled together. After beating their mother, Jim left. Maria crawled out of the bed and ran to the window to watch and make sure he had gone. As he drove off, she memorized his license plate number. She kept repeating it over and over as she paced in the room. Her mother was covered in blood from her beating and lay on the floor, semiconscious.

It wasn't long before Maria could hear sirens. The police came in, with George Jr. and Jake running to lead them. When the police arrived and took a statement, they asked Anna if she knew the man. "I thought he liked me. I stayed with him a couple of nights. I only asked him for a ride to the liquor store. He didn't have to treat me like that. He should be in jail."

The police officer looked around the house and at the kids. Maria trusted him and walked forward. "ABC 1D3," she said.

He looked at her again. "What did you say?"

She repeated, "ABC 1D3."

He understood. "That's the license number?"

Maria nodded.

"Thank you. You're a smart little girl."

Maria didn't grin. She had tried to focus on other things during the evening with Jim, and now, it finally overwhelmed her. She was exhausted.

When the police left, Anna went to bed. Gertruda tried to crawl in bed with her, but she kicked her out. "Get away from me, you stupid whore. Go to your own bed."

Gertruda was crushed. She walked to the metal twin bed that she shared with her sister, and they both went to bed.

Maria took a long time to get to sleep. She was still doing the math in her head and wished so much that she could go to school. She decided that the next day, she would get up early and catch the bus.

The next morning, Maria was up in the dark, looking for clothes for school. She found some from her last foster home that she really liked, and they were clean. She put on the shirt and pants and found some shoes that fit before walking to the road in the dark and waiting for the bus. As she waited, the sun came up, and she was pleased she had picked such warm clothes. Her pants had flowers on them and matched the shirt perfectly. They were soft and new flannel. She was very proud to wear them and thought the kids would like them too. She huddled under the October sky, waiting, and finally, the bus came. She proudly walked to the door, past the driver, and to the back of the bus to sit down. All the kids turned to look at her. She had never taken the bus on her own before, but she knew the routines and how it all worked because of her times in foster care. She was so proud to be there that morning. She got off the bus and went with the others into the school in a line. She liked fitting in. She went to the first room and found a chair. The teacher looked at her and asked for her name.

"Maria," she said. "Take my hand and let's have a walk. Are you new to this school? What grade are you in?"

Maria shook her head no. She felt like she was going to be in trouble and not allowed to stay at school. She started to panic. All she wanted to do was go to school. They walked to the principal's office, and she stood in front of the big desk.

"Tell me where you live," the principal asked. Maria shrugged. She didn't know. "Tell me if your mom or dad is home or where they work." Maria said nothing. She thought being quiet was the best way to get to stay in school that day. The bell rang, and all the kids shuffled in the hallway. She just wanted to go with the kids and fit in. She went to walk to the hallway and leave the office, but the teacher stopped her.

"I have to go to my class. You stay here with Principal White."

Maria was given a chair to sit on and a book while the principal made several phone calls. She didn't mind because it felt like school, and she was doing what she wanted. A few minutes later, a police officer came into the office. He sat next to her and asked her, "Who helped dress you this morning?" Maria proudly

CHAPTER SEVENTEEN: HOPE AND NEW BEGINNINGS

stated she had dressed herself in her best outfit. "These are your pajamas," he said. "They're very nice. Did your mom make you breakfast this morning?"

Maria shook her head no. "My mom is sleeping."

"Where is Dad?" Maria shrugged. She didn't know. "We need to get you home for today."

Maria was upset and started to cry. "I just want to go to school."

"I know. Let's try and do it better tomorrow." The principal got some toast for Maria as the police officer talked to her. Maria gobbled up the toast as the two watched her. She didn't want to go home. She wanted a different life than that.

He put her in the cruiser and drove her home. She pointed to where the house was, and then he pulled into the driveway. George Jr., Jake, and Gertruda were outside playing, and Peter and John were in the house. He knocked on the door, which brought all the kids running. "Is Maria in trouble?" The kids were laughing.

"I was here last night too," the officer said. As George Jr. and Jake recounted the story of the evening before, Anna opened the front door.

"Get off my property. You don't touch my kids." She grabbed Maria by the shoulder and pulled her into the house.

"Your daughter went to school today. Did you know that?"

Anna looked at Maria and slapped her across the back of the head. "She has no right to run off like that."

"No, it's okay. All your children should be going to school, but she's in pajamas, and her hair is full of dirt. When was the last time you gave the kids a bath?" He looked over all of the children.

"That's none of your business. We don't have a water tub here to bathe the kids and only cold water from the well. I don't have no man to help me around here."

"You have to do better. Is there family you could call to come and help you or that I could go and get? Where's your husband?"

"You're not going to get my family here. They're always mad at me. My husband is in town with a new woman. He doesn't think I'm good enough and doesn't provide for us. He lets his kids starve. You arrest him and leave us alone. Get off my property."

He walked to his cruiser and called CAS, waiting at the end of the lane for them to arrive. They came to the house with the officer and told Anna that she needed to let them in to see the home. Anna began yelling and punching, and the officer had to move her out of the doorway and to the police car. The children all watched with interest.

The social worker walked into the home, horrified at what she saw. Mice and rats were on the kitchen counters. The weak board in the floor had now broken through completely, and the hole was full of rainwater. The stove was only sitting on a few boards and would soon fall through. She walked to the bedroom and found a large pile of clothing about six feet deep. On the edges of the pile were smaller piles of clothing laid out into beds where the children would sleep if it was a cold night. The roof panels, made of old tin, were beginning to fall in due to roof damage. Rain had soaked the clothing, leaving everything musty and moldy.

She walked into the next room, where the old chalkboards were still on the wall. There were three beds and a crib in there. The mattresses were filthy with dirt, feces, and urine. There were no sheets or pillows, just more old clothing used as a blanket. The yard held a working well but also a large pile of stool-soiled clothing from diapers and kids soiling their underclothes. They would just throw them into a pile behind the house. There was no heat, and there were no lights in the house, as all the bulbs were burned out, but the stove did work.

The routines of having police and social work move them from house to house was part of the children's lives by this point. Usually, they went in pairs, and they were never sure when they would see each other again whenever they left. They would all make eye contact and silently nod goodbyes to each other. Anna would be left alone in the house with the social worker, reviewing all the steps needed to get the children returned. She would sit, dazed, watching her children go and appreciating the peace and quiet that drowned out the social worker's voice.

This time, Maria was taken by herself to live with a family on a farm. She wasn't sure where the rest of her family went. There was another girl in the house, and they were expecting a baby. She shared a room with the other girl. This wasn't a Mennonite house, so it was very different for her. There were lots of toys, a television, and music. She got to spend a lot of time outside. She chased geese, who then chased her back, and learned the hard pinch of a duck's

CHAPTER SEVENTEEN: HOPE AND NEW BEGINNINGS

bill if you got too close too fast. They had kittens there too. It was a nice, stress-free place to live. It reminded her of her short time in Mexico, and that gave her some comfort.

The other girl was older than Maria and wanted to talk a lot about boys.

"Do you think the neighbour boy likes me? See how he looks at me?" Kelly asked.

Maria had never thought of this type of relationship before. She watched the boy play with his stick, kick balls, and run. She couldn't tell if he was even aware that they were in the same yard. She nodded, though, knowing that if she gave a wrong opinion, living in the house would be harder for her.

The family was preparing for the birth of their baby, including decorating the bedroom. Maria and Kelly went with the mother to an ultrasound appointment. Maria had never seen a naked pregnant belly, and the size horrified her. She stood in the corner of the room as the ultrasound technician ran lubricant and a wand over the mother's stomach. Maria could only wonder how it was so big and how she could lie there and have others look at it. She felt ashamed for the mother and kept her eyes on the floor.

"Look here, girls. That's the baby moving, and that's its heartbeat." Kelly ran closer to look and touch her mother's stomach. Maria stayed back, not looking up, but she listened to the heartbeat. It was against God to expose yourself to strangers. There was no way that she should be part of it. She kept her head down and didn't speak of it again on the drive home. She wasn't sure where babies came from, but there was some shame associated with it, and she wanted to distance herself.

When they got home, the father had bought a new tent trailer. Kelly and Maria could sleep in it in the yard if they wanted to. Kelly ran out to see it, very excited about camping trips. Maria tentatively walked out to it. It was made of canvas and steel, and when she went in, she was surprised that it had beds and a table in it. This little house was clean and tidy, and she was pleased with it. She took off her shoes and crawled into the double bed on one side of the trailer, Kelly doing the same on the other side. Maria lay back and looked at the sun through the canvas and screen. She touched the fabric and decided it was almost like touching the clouds.

Kelly was bouncing around and opening cupboards. She yelled for the neighbour boys to come and see the new trailer. Maria wished they would go away. She'd had enough of her brothers with their yelling and wrestling, and this was a rare peaceful moment for her. She had so few of them and was sad when the three boys came bouncing into the trailer and onto the beds. Maria curled into a corner and tried to focus on just seeing the clouds and hearing nothing, becoming invisible. The boys saw and asked Kelly about her.

"She lives with us because she's poor and her parents don't want her." Kelly laughed, and the boys all turned to look at Maria.

"She's not that bad, but she doesn't say anything. Is she slow?" The boys laughed.

"Yes, she's probably slow," Kelly stated as she also laughed. They stood staring at Maria.

Maria could no longer ignore them. She got up without saying anything and went outside to walk to the barn. They let her pass and eagerly jumped onto her bed on the other side of the tent trailer.

Maria found the changes hard, but she knew how much harder it was to be at home. She just wanted peace and quiet. Sitting on a wagon's edge, the kittens came to her. She had barn cats coming up and rubbing against her. She loved every one of them, seeing kindness and caring in their eyes. She was gentle with them, enjoying every moment alone. It was hard with her own family to ever have time without stress, siblings, looking for food, and not knowing where her parents were. At foster homes, you had new rules, new families, and you never belonged, but she tried to be grateful. She repeated in her head, *You need to love the cats today and the clouds. Tomorrow, you may have none.*

Her foster mother yelled from the yard that supper was ready. She ran toward the house just as Kelly and the three boys came out of the trailer, running.

"You guys better go home. See you after," Kelly said, smiling. The boys waved at her as she caught up with Maria, running to the house. One boy picked up a rock and threw it, hitting Maria between the shoulder blades. She winced but kept running even faster. She'd lived with more pain that that in her life, and she could outrun them if she had to.

She got to the door first. Both of the parents were home for dinner. The father wasn't often there, as he was in the military reserves and working. "Get in there and wash your hands before dinner," he yelled. Maria obediently walked to the washroom to wash her hands, but Kelly sat at the table.

"I'm not dirty. I don't need to wash."

CHAPTER SEVENTEEN: HOPE AND NEW BEGINNINGS

He raised his voice. "Get in there and do what Maria is doing, NOW."

Kelly grunted and pushed her chair back to walk to the washroom. Maria was on her way back to the table. "I hate you," Kelly said.

Maria looked into her eyes, and they seemed darker. She hadn't been afraid of Kelly before, but she was now. She went to the table and sat with her head down.

"Did you have fun outside playing?" he asked. Maria nodded her head. Kelly quickly returned to the table and pulled her chair in. "What were you doing outside, Kelly?"

"Maria and I were playing in the new camper with the Smith brothers. It's really nice. Can we sleep in it tonight?"

"I hope you didn't get it dirty," said her mother.

Kelly reassured them that everyone took their shoes off. They ate dinner. It was pasta and sauce, but Maria had never had pasta before. She tasted the noodles, and they were tangy and slippery. She gagged on the first mouthful. Everyone at the table turned to look at her. Her face flushed, and she looked down. She didn't like everyone looking at her. She put another forkful of food in the mouth and started to dry heave. She swallowed hard.

"What's your problem?" the father asked her.

Maria didn't want him to be angry. She ate again, and this time, she could swallow it. The combination of texture and tartness made her struggle with the food. She said nothing.

He continued to watch her, and Kelly snickered as she ate. Maria couldn't finish all her dinner. "You don't leave until your plate is empty. Do you hear me?" he said.

Maria's eyes welled up with tears. He got up and pushed his chair back firmly and walked into the adjoining living room, where he had a tripod with a gun on it. He kept it in the living room when he was home from his military reserve training. He turned the gun toward Maria and spoke, looking into her tear-filled eyes. "Eat your dinner, now. Don't make me use this gun."

She had never seen a gun before, but she knew from his expression that it was meant to hurt her. Kelly sat frozen in her chair, looking at him.

Finally, the mother said, "Stop that. Let her eat in peace. If she's not hungry, she can just leave the table."

He got up and went to the table again. "Get out of my sight," he said to Maria. She got up and went to her room, shaking as she walked. She hated it when she made people unhappy, worried that they would hit her. She lay on the floor and slid under the bed. He wouldn't find her there. Her heart was racing, and she could feel the food coming back up from her stomach. She held her mouth shut with, her eyes watering, and swallowed again. Curled up tight, she lay very quietly, barely breathing, and fell asleep.

"What are you doing under the bed, Maria?" the mother asked.

Maria opened her eyes to see the mother looking at her. She felt comforted by this look and reached for her outstretched hand to be helped out from under the bed. Kelly was sitting on her bed already, smiling at Maria.

"Let's get you guys into the tub, and then you can sleep outside in the camper tonight."

"I'm afraid to sleep outside. Can I just stay in my bed?" Maria quietly asked.

The mother looked at her and nodded. "Kelly, you can't sleep out there alone, so we won't be in the camper tonight."

"What?! Just because she won't sleep outside, I can't? That's not fair. She needs to go. Then, I can do what I want."

Kelly's mother touched her arm and said, "Stop. Don't talk like that. Maybe your father will sleep outside with you." Hopeful, Kelly decided to ask him. The mother walked to the washroom to run a bath. Her abdomen was large with pregnancy, and it was hard for her to bend. She would let Kelly bathe first, then Maria.

Kelly and Maria finished their bath. The father told them to stay in their towels for inspection. He sat in the living room on the sofa with his gun near him. He motioned for them to come over. "Open your towel and show me that you're clean." Kelly bounced toward her father and opened her towel. He had her drop the towel and turn around. "Yup. Good job. You're clean. Get your pajamas on." "Daddy, will you sleep with me in the new camper tonight? Maria won't go, and I really, really want to sleep in it."

"Yes. Let's do it. Get your flashlight and things gathered up."

Maria walked toward the father. "Open your towel, Maria, and drop it." She did as she was told and could feel his eyes looking at her naked body. She focused on the wall behind him and listened to the mother at the sink, washing dishes. She just wanted to be covered. She knew what some men wanted from her and

CHAPTER SEVENTEEN: HOPE AND NEW BEGINNINGS

didn't want to give it. "Turn around." She did. "Okay, pretty girl. Get your pajamas on. Are you okay to sleep alone in the bedroom if Kelly sleeps outside?"

Maria nodded and quickly grabbed her towel to cover herself. She was shivering, frightened, and just wanted to hide. She had never slept in a bed alone. Sometimes, in foster homes, she and Gertruda would get their own beds, but she always had company in the room.

CHAPTER EIGHTEEN:
LIVES IN PIECES

1970

George was trying hard to be part of his new community, find his place, and succeed, but it had its challenges. Learning English and finding the right words for situations to fit in were the hardest parts. At the bar, after a few drinks, everyone spoke so much faster and started using words that he had never heard before. He would laugh with the crowd on occasion to appear like he understood, but there were many slang and swear words that he could never remember long enough to ask others what they meant.

Tootsie would wait for him after work finished, and they would share a drink before he slept in the back room. He wouldn't often go home. He didn't want to go home anymore. He liked his children, but he knew he was a disappointment to them. He couldn't help Anna. All he could focus on was working and getting enough money saved for a better life. He was still of the mindset that it was Anna's job to raise the children as it was in Mexico and with the Mennonites, but Anna was never able to fulfill that role, and his lack of acceptance of her abilities had led his children to a life of constant disruptions and chaos.

He wanted a new beginning, and Tootsie gave him hope for that. He was gentle around her, and she admired his strong arms and shoulders. He had never smiled as much as when he was with her in his entire life. He felt free for once.

In the meantime, the social workers were working with Anna and George to try and get their children back to their home. Anna was running around with

CHAPTER EIGHTEEN: LIVES IN PIECES

other men when the children were away, and George's infrequent stops at the house didn't allow them to cross paths. He tried to fix the floors and get the power back on again, but everything cost money. He was private about his wife and children at the hotel. He didn't want them judging him at this early stage of his life in Ontario. He tried to find a few people to trust, and they would lend him tools to fix the house and get it ready. It took several months before the CAS found Anna and George suitable enough to get their children back, and they would receive weekly check-ins from social workers to see if they were being good parents. Anna had now gotten on welfare and was getting some money thanks to the social workers, who also supervised her meal preparation for the children. They wrote letters to the landlord to help George fix the house. They still had to carry water into the house, but at least they managed to get the roof repaired to keep the weather out. Electricity was connected, and the stove would now work so they could make food. They repaired the refrigerator, and they found clean bedding from the Mennonite thrift shop in Aylmer for the beds. The house was in as good a shape as it could be, and Anna and George had worked together to make this happen. They were beginning to understand that some government workers could work with you and not be a threat to you as they had been raised to believe.

When the kids were all picked up from their various foster homes and taken home, they were excited to see each other and share stories of their time while they were away. They hadn't seen each other for months, so it was a big reunion for each of them. But at the same time, every foster home gave them a different perception on life and the world around them, changing each of them and driving them further apart. Even though they were all together now, they felt very alone, enduring their own experiences in silence. In foster care, they faced abuse—emotional, sexual, and physical—and the feelings of being second-class and never being part of any family.

Anna had a hot meal on the stove. It was small pork roast and potatoes. She was so happy to see her kids. She appreciated the independence of having no children, but she also liked to just look at them and know they came from her. Her actions weren't always in line with what God wanted, but seeing them was her reward. The voices in Anna's head were constantly criticizing her these days, and her confidence was low because of it. She had slowed down her drinking as the social workers had requested and was trying to get into a routine at home so that her children could be happy.

George was there to greet them. He was quiet around them and watched them play. He could see they weren't his Mennonite children anymore. They were more Canadian than he ever thought his kids would be. They spoke fluent English, they didn't have the same chores that he had as a kid that would have given them discipline and structure, and they didn't have any friends or cousins to play with. It was hard for him to watch as they got their plates full of food.

Anna handed him a plate, and he met her eyes. She had combed her hair and was in a clean dress. He remembered her briefly as an innocent young girl. They had both changed so much over their marriage. He could no longer say he had any affection for her. He knew what it was like to truly love someone now, and he longed to be part of another life with another woman and raise his children with her instead.

Anna had never been allowed to be in charge of money. Now, with the monthly cheque coming in, she would eagerly wait for its arrival, and when it came in the mail, she would go away for a week or more. She now had a bank account of her own, and this gave her a great sense of accomplishment. She would put some money in the account but then go back daily to take it out in small portions until it was gone in a matter of weeks. She didn't understand balancing budgets or even counting physical money. She would put all her money on the counter for her purchases and trust that the cashier would give her back the right change. Mennonite women could certainly manage money in a home, but she had never gotten to that stage in her marriage, as George knew she wasn't reliable enough to save and use it for running the home.

Knowing that Anna had a cheque of her own now, George was sending less money home to her, as he was trying to save. He felt reassured that with the support of the social workers, she would learn to spend money on the right items to keep their children healthy. But only a few weeks after the children came home, Anna started going into town again, looking for company. She felt independent and confident with a few dollars of her own. She started going away one night at a time again and would always miss the social worker visits. They were keeping track; the children were again not attending school regularly.

Still, Anna felt free as a bird. The voices were still part of her life, but she could shut some of them down if they were too negative and try and negotiate

CHAPTER EIGHTEEN: LIVES IN PIECES

with the others. She enjoyed the voices when they told her what she deserved in life, and it fueled her to start drinking again.

She would disappear for a few days and then return intermittently with various men to drop off oatmeal or bread, but not always.

The power bill was never paid, and it was cut off yet again. The winter was cold, and the kids were running out of ways to stay warm. They would often all curl up together under loose clothing to be warm for the day. The baby John would cry a lot. Johnny needed diaper changes, and Maria and Gertruda tried their best to do it. Anger was growing in the kids. They would fight more and not trust each other. Someone took more food or more blankets than others. No one was going to school anymore. It was about survival. George and Anna were living their own lives, hoping that the support system in Ontario would pick up the pieces where they were failing as parents.

This behaviour would cycle until Anna made the walk on the cold and snowy night to her brother Gerhard's house, on the night yet another man had assaulted her and George had found her and the children without food and her covered in bruises. It seemed that patterns were not being broken, and something had to change.

Unfortunately, George would never see that change come. On the night of January 2, 1972, all the problems culminated in a premeditated shooting, its coverup, and the separation of his and Anna's family.

The home of Gerhard Wolf

CHAPTER NINETEEN:
AFTER THE TRIAL

Immediately after the shooting, Anna stayed at Gerhard and Margaret's home with the children until after the funeral, when CAS social workers came and removed them. After that, they were all placed into foster homes.

Gerhard was accused of murdering George, and the Mennonite women in the Wolf house had no income; this combination would impact the lives of the children in the house. In preparation for the trial, Gerhard was coached to reinforce the facts as presented by the Wolf family and church elders. After the trial and Gerhard's release, he returned to his home.

Anna was there, full of anger and resentment because of what her brother did to her husband and how he had her children taken away. She was incredibly stressed and resorted to her same pattern of behaviour, seeking alcohol for sexual favours. She went missing for days on end, and she brought men to his home. She was seen wandering the streets of Aylmer and St. Thomas, seeking men and alcohol from anyone who would be available. Gerhard eventually had her committed to the St. Thomas Psychiatric Hospital. During this time, I'm confident he would have had ample time to reflect on the stories his sister had told him and doubt his reasoning for pulling the trigger on his brother-in-law and best friend.

Through the CAS, Anna was allowed to bring gifts to her children in foster care but not see them. She made a hand-sewn quilt from old clothing for Gertruda's and Maria's (my) dolls. It's unclear if any items were delivered to the

CHAPTER NINETEEN: AFTER THE TRIAL

other children. Anna remained in the psychiatric hospital for over a year until her sister from Mexico came and asked Gerhard where Anna was. This sister, Maria, would then get her out of the hospital. With limited English and no money to speak of, the two sisters would drink together in St. Thomas, and Anna's addiction began again.

Following the trial, Anna's mother, Maria, would also come to Canada from Mexico. She lived in Leamington, and Anna found a way to her home and stayed with her for a short time.

However, her behaviour was unacceptable, and she was kicked out. Soon after that, her mother died. Anna deeply felt the loss of her mother. Their relationship was always strained, but she felt a connection to her and felt that her mother had a deep understanding of Anna and her voices.

Anna was able to find an apartment in the area. By this point, Jake had aged out of foster care. He found Anna and lived with her for a short time. He was able to get a disability pension due to his intellectual disabilities and helped pay the rent with his mother. However, neither of them were familiar with managing budgets, and soon, all the money was spent, and Anna was having men in the apartment for sex and drinks. It was then that Jake decided to leave. He hitchhiked as far as he could go and ended up in a small southern Ontario town, working in a garage as a handyman. He loved this work.

Anna eventually ended up homeless on the streets of Windsor. She resumed her addictions and lived with others who she called "family." I found her through leaving my name at the Mission in Windsor, a shelter for the homeless to get meals and stay warm at night. I had contacted her sister after getting information from the Aylmer Mennonite CC office, and she had stated Anna was homeless. The Mennonite community no longer accepted Anna and her behaviour and effectively turned their backs on her.

My first meeting with Anna after being placed in foster care that final time was at the Mission. We shared a coffee in a large room with many other people present. She looked nothing like I remembered her, but what made me confident it was her was her dark brown eyes and her smile. She had shoulder-length grey hair, no teeth, and was dressed in many layers of heavily soiled clothing. She kept her hands on a two-wheeled cart that contained her belongings. She mumbled about being robbed and that she only had a bit of stuff left. She looked at me with no recognition.

NOT MY KIND OF MENNONITE

I introduced myself to her, and she shook her head no. "I don't have any kids anymore." My hopes for a more fulfilling reunion were soon dispelled, and I had more flashbacks to our lives together. She spoke in scrambled sentences, expressing random thoughts and paranoid behaviours, always looking over her shoulder and keeping a tight grip on her cart. I reminded her of how we were connected, and she shook her head no each time. I named all her children, and when I said "Gertruda," she stopped. She looked at me again and asked, "Where is my Gertruda?" I told her she was safe in a group home. My mother then went back to her thoughts and voices as I sat and witnessed her crinkle plastic bags to find a glass bottle of Crown Royal and drink the remaining liquid.

Our visit was short. I wanted to leave the room. I had tucked away the abuse and trauma of many years inside me, and now, they were opening up again. My hate was growing, and I knew I had to leave her. I left my name at the Mission in the event Anna needed clothing or had health concerns. At this time, I asked her if she wanted help finding her own place. She adamantly said, "No. These people are my family." In the depths of her misery, she had discovered true friends, the ones she met on the street. She was still an alcoholic and had very few possessions except those which fit into her cart.

For over ten years, Anna lived on the streets. I visited about twice a year. Each time, I was stronger and more courageous in talking with her about the past. I wanted to know if she loved my father. She always said, "I tricked him into marrying me, and I loved him, but he never loved me." She shared brief moments of clarity before disappearing to the fights inside her head and soul. She even had me meet a few of her partners on the street, and I brought food and snacks to her. I once brought a new coat for her, but even when I was still within sight, she traded it for a bottle of clear liquid from another homeless acquaintance.

One December, I received a phone call that my mother had "fallen and broken both of her arms." At this time, my "mother" was my adoptive mother—I never referred to Anna as my mother, so I was confused, as my adoptive mother didn't drink, but I soon understood that it was Anna who had two broken arms.

The hospital eventually placed her in a nursing home, where she would fit in very well. With medication, regular meals, and proper housing, she started to smile again during our visits and eventually remembered things from her life. I brought Gertruda and Jacob with me for visits, and she shared stories. We bought clothing for her and took her to a restaurant for a meal, which always

CHAPTER NINETEEN: AFTER THE TRIAL

included pie. You could get her to talk about her youth, baking, and living in Mexico, and she would have flashes of abuse and loneliness that she would share. She revealed her own sexual abuse, her beatings, and her feelings of disappointing everyone. She eventually improved enough to remember who we were and could share some more stories. She still loved that Gertruda looked just like her. She just sat and smiled at her. She asked how my labours were with my own children. She teared up when she talked about George and his shooting. She often said that he never loved her. She said that she was "slow" and that he was ashamed of her. She was probably right.

It was during these few moments of clarity that I began to realize that Anna functioned at about a Grade 2 level of understanding and comprehension. She couldn't read or write, which I attributed to her Mennonite upbringing, but it was more than that. I had to stop and reflect on my childhood trauma and then wonder realistically how a woman with these barriers, including schizophrenia, could have possibly raised six children. Due to her mental illness and addictions, she suffered after the death of two children and from the lack of ability to organize her home and life. She needed her colony to help her, and yet they kept their distance because of the shame she brought to them and their church. Her colony didn't want to help her if her behaviour was far from acceptable in their congregation, and she was "not willing to help herself."

Most of her stories were about the men she had met in her life, and then out of the blue, she would cry and say, "Why did he have to shoot my husband? Took all you kids away." She was still trying to get bottles of alcohol from us when we came to visit, but she enjoyed her life of bowling, crafts, and relationships that the nursing home provided her. Her sisters and other family members rarely had contact with her, so other than the people at the nursing home, her children were her only company.

At the age of sixty-six, Anna's life of COPD, diabetes, and alcohol abuse caused her to be short of breath and required her to be in the ICU on a ventilator. The medical team asked for all her children to come in and say our goodbyes, as they were going to withdraw life support. Her lungs were so damaged from smoking over the years, and she'd had so many small heart attacks with her lifestyle and her diabetes, that recovery wasn't expected. My number was the contact number they had, and I did my best to notify my siblings and try to get their consensus on our mother's end-of-life care. In the end, all her children came to say goodbye to her.

We crowded around her bed as the medical team discussed the steps, and they allowed each of us to speak to her. They took her off her ventilator, and she kept breathing. It was such a hard thing to have every child present with a mother that had subjected them to such unspeakable abuse, and yet we wanted to see her one more time. She didn't die that day, but all the children went home after their goodbyes. This had been the first time her two youngest children, Peter and John, had seen their mother since they were put up for adoption. They had only scant memories of their lives with her but felt it was important to see her for the last time.

Later that night, I got a phone call saying they were moving Anna back to the nursing home to die, as they needed the ICU bed. I needed to go in and sign a do-not-resuscitate order for the nursing home. It was with some anger and frustration that I drove back to Windsor to sign these papers; Anna was taking yet another day to complicate my life. I struggled with balancing my obligations as a daughter and nurse to Anna and my memories of the trauma she exposed me to as a child. I felt a pain in my stomach and chest as I tried to calm myself and make the right decisions for this woman who had spent many years suffering.

When I arrived to see her in her bed, I could tell by her breathing that she wouldn't live long, so I decided to stay with her. I spoke gently to her. I watched her breathe, looked at her small hands, facial wrinkles, and grey hair, and I reflected on the life that she lived. It was overwhelmingly sad to think of how this woman suffered with sexual abuse, addictions, generational trauma, and a faith that turned its back on her for experiencing all that. I bathed her, as she was very sweaty and working hard to die. I reached into her bedside table to find a comb or brush and heard glass bottles hitting each other. I moved a few items aside and found multiple small sizes of Crown Royal in all her drawers. I held one in my hand and looked at her. Addictions are so very powerful, and combined with mental illness, abuse, and trauma, they're almost impossible to overcome. The company of the bottle got her through so many hardships.

I found a brush for her hair and gently pulled the grey strands behind her ears. She always had such lovely long hair, I recalled. I found lotion in her drawer for her feet and hands. Her bedside table had a few photos we had given her

CHAPTER NINETEEN: AFTER THE TRIAL

over the years of our children and her grandchildren. I reinforced that she did all she could, and we were now all adults in charge of our own lives. I thanked her for life and allowing me to have a wonderful family of my own.

She breathed more rapidly and become more distressed. In my years of experience with the dying, I recognized that she might have been holding on for my sake and didn't want to die with me present. I decided to leave the room and get a drink. In the few minutes I was gone, she had stopped breathing and died. She died alone, just as she had spent most of her life. Her fight was over. She could finally rest. She was forgiven and understood.

Her remaining immediate family was notified of her death. I had considered burying her with her mother in the Mennonite cemetery, but that was forbidden due to her lifestyle choices. Her ashes stayed in my home for several years as my siblings and I tried to find the most meaningful resting place for her. She needed to be placed back to the earth, and so now, she is buried with her husband and brother in St. Luke's cemetery, Vienna, Ontario.

Gertruda spent a short time in foster care, but with added rules and boundaries around her behaviour, she rebelled. She was accustomed to being the oldest, the one who helped her mother, and there was no family for her to take care of here. She set fires and also started prostituting. She aged out of foster care and was in and out of jail. At the age of twenty she was sent to Barrie to the Edgar Adult Occupational Centre to learn life skills and live in the residential housing. Gertruda would reside there for four years. She would shorten her name to Gerda which she preferred. Gertruda was sterilizated during her stay at Edgar. She was raped on multiple occasions by residents and staff during her stay and often described her life as "horrible and lonely" there. She was released when the government of Ontario was eliminating many of these types of residences for disabled persons.

She was moved to a group home in a small town in Ontario, and that was where she finally met her siblings once again. Through all the years, she asked many times to find her family, and finally, she did. Her records from Edgar Adult Occupational Centre never acknowledged that she had been abused in her past or that her mother was still alive. Gertruda reads and writes at about a Grade One level . She had counselling for many years for her PTSD and rapes, but ultimately, the damage stayed with her forever. She loves a sunny beach day and can rarely remember a story from her childhood or time in the institution, but that's okay Her body is now protecting her by not giving her flash backs and rare triggers to her abuse and neglect. She's now an aunt and a great-aunt, and she's supported and cared for.

As I mentioned earlier, after living with Anna, Jacob hitchhiked to a small town and worked in a garage as a handyman for many years. Local people helped him with budgeting, finding an apartment, and building a life. He loved everything to do with repairing engines. He could read and write and finished Grade 10 at high school. One random night, George Jr. delivered auto parts to a garage, where he ran into his brother, Jacob That was how he met up with his siblings again. He worked various jobs during his life in vegetable processing and bagging firewood. He works hard and continues to struggle with budgeting and money management. He enjoys a good scratch/lotto ticket, car race, and documentary. He lives alone; he has tried to live with others but found that he prefers his own space.

George Jr. also aged out of foster care and came to live in the St. Thomas area. He married and had four children and is a very successful mechanic. He is a stunning likeness of his father in appearance and stature.

The youngest three children—Peter, John, and I—were put up for adoption in July of 1973. At the time, there was no social work interview to assess our sexual, physical, and emotional abuse. The adoptive parents were counselled by social workers to "start fresh" and not bring up anything from the children's past. The courage this childless couple living a quiet farm life possessed to take three emotionally and physically abused children was enormous. Over the years, they began to understand the depth of this trauma. Their own love and support couldn't cover everything, but they remained devoted to raising their children as their own. This was the foundation we desperately needed.

When I shared my family history with another Mennonite woman, she shook her head and said, "You are not my kind of Mennonite." This simple phrase brought me such clarity about the struggles my parents and other Mennonites have had.

To the public, the word "Mennonite" brings up visions of high-quality foods and furniture, as well as homemade quilts and clothing. This image has become a marketing strategy to provide them the financial means to maintain their

CHAPTER NINETEEN: AFTER THE TRIAL

"traditional way of life." Mennonites continue to be pilgrims to other countries until this day. They seek a place of isolation to remain devoted to the teaching of God and maintain the longevity of the faith. The numerous groups and schisms that formed from the original Mennonite organization over hundreds of years signifies the changes they have made in adapting to the world around them. Each community establishes their own identities while still being bound together in a similar faith. Some congregations have gone farther south to Bolivia and Paraguay to achieve the utopian Biblical society away from law and control of governments. Others run successful businesses of farmers' markets and thrive in communities, making large profits.

When George and Anna succumbed to their struggles of integrating into a non-Mennonite community with no support from family and friends, they were cast aside by the faith. Both George and Anna suffered abuse, neglect, religious pressures, and excommunication in their lives, and their parents before them potentially experienced the same. The effect of being turned away by the only community you know is life-changing. Many secrets and a lot of shame has been transmitted through Mennonite families and suppressed due to fear of shunning and social isolation. This process impacts their children's lives and predisposes others to continued trauma.

This book was written as a legacy to my father. His voice wasn't heard at his murder trial. No one stood in his defense for the man he was and wanted to become. He stood tall and proud and always had a smile. He tried to fit into a new life and was succeeding when he was killed. I hope that in the darkness of his death, he achieved the freedom he was seeking. If I see only suffering in the life and death of my father, then I'm doing him an injustice as one of his survivors. He left, as his legacy, sons and daughters who carry the burden of trying to find answers where there are none, but also the strength to live a life that would make him proud. His immigration story, hard work, and perseverance are in all his descendants, as are his eyes, comically large ears, and smile.

Anna grew to understand and feel compassion and acceptance in her later years of life, as she was treated with medication to soothe the voices that plagued her. She became Anna with a gentle smile and a mischievous sparkle in her eye, and she was a mother and grandmother when she died.

It took a lot of courage for George and Anna to venture away from their community and pursue a life of their own invention. Through their end-of-life journeys, there must have been a moment of letting go of all the mistakes and what-ifs as they died. I hope that in this process, they were able to fully appreciate and love what they had experienced, good or bad. Their paths to death were not Biblical, but I hope there was some peace and self-forgiveness.

> "Religion is for those that fear hell; spirituality is for those that have been there."
>
> —David Bowie

I come from a long line of spiritualists. From the hardships and trauma of life, one can peel back the layers and reveal the reality that life was never designed to be fair. How we choose to own it, process it, and then move forward can make all the difference.

Anna and Gertruda in Windsor, Ontario

CHAPTER TWENTY:
ANALYSIS OF NEWSPAPER ARTICLES AND TRIAL

January 3, 1972

Margaret and Anna were on their own in the farmhouse with twelve children. George was dead, and Gerhard had turned himself in to the police for killing his friend. The older children knew what had happened, and the others knew, because of the tears and tension, that life would never be the same again.

Anna wasn't coping well with the death of her husband. She knew that what had happened to him was tragic and that he didn't deserve to be killed. At the same time, she was unable to recognize how her behaviour could have anything to do with his death. Margaret started coaching her then about how awful George was as a husband and how afraid she was of him. They had to get their stories straight to get Gerhard out of jail. Neither one of them was working; each was getting a government cheque, but the house was part of the greenhouse, and Margaret couldn't stay there if there was no husband to work. Her older children were almost old enough to work in his place. The elders of the church who were visiting Margaret and her family were working with the crown attorneys to help Gerhard.

The police had come to the house during the day to show crime scene photographs to Anna and her older children. Anna refused to look at them, as she felt too upset, and she left the room crying. It was George Jr. and Jacob who identified their father lying outside the car, blue, frozen, and with blood on the snow beside him. Maria caught sight of the photo as the police officer talked to the older boys. She wasn't sure it if was real. It didn't look real. It didn't look like her father.

The police had called CAS on the night of George's murder. They saw that with no men in the home and the mothers not working, it would be a challenge for all the children to stay. All of George and Anna's children were taken into foster homes within the week following the murder.

Gerhard's brother John sent a telegram to Jacob and Gertruda Peters, George's parents, in Mexico to let them know their son had been killed. They arranged to buy a car, and they drove to Ontario for their son's funeral. However, there were delays at the Detroit border crossing, causing them to be a day late for his funeral and burial. Other relatives and members of the Old Colony congregation would sit vigil with George's body and his family.

On the day of the funeral at the Old Colony Mennonite church, the children were seated around the coffin to see their father. They all sat motionless and quiet on the wooden benches of the church. They were dressed in dark, traditional Mennonite clothing and looked at the body of their father in the wooden box. He almost didn't look real or even dead as he lay there. There was mumbling in the church, but no one was speaking. The minister at the Old Colony Mennonite church led the service. Aunt Margaret whispered in Maria's ear, "It's okay to cry, you know."

Anna sobbed next to her, not making any eye contact with the children. She was very upset and now a widow. She didn't understand why her husband was dead or how her life was going to move forward with no husband. It was all a blur to her. She had seen other women in the colony become widows, and she knew how she should act. She also knew that crying publicly was very frowned upon in the community. Open displays of grief were meant to be done in front of family or privately, and yet she couldn't stop sobbing. She could only think of how her husband's death would affect her. She couldn't understand why her brother had killed her husband.

The children sat with heads lowered. The older boys were numb with disbelief that their father had been killed. They could feel anger, hatred, and revenge in their hearts as they saw their uncle Gerhard sitting in the church with his police escort waiting outside. He was allowed to attend from jail. Gertruda nervously looked at her mother and how her heavy sobs echoed in the church. She could feel her mother's pain and wished that she would make her laugh again. She was unable to cry. Maria watched her father in the coffin and waited for him to open his eyes. He had a grin that would cause his ears to lift, and she only wanted to see that now. She stared, barely blinking, at him for any sign that he was still alive.

Gerhard sat next to his wife, Margaret, and both took quick glances around the church and then to Anna. They needed the support of the congregation to get through the next few months and felt that sitting together and supporting George's family was the best they could do in the circumstances. Gerhard sat and looked at his friend in the coffin. They had shared so many hopes and dreams in their lives. He could feel tension in his throat and chest as he fought off the tears, but then, he let go, and he quietly cried.

Summary of the Case

The research into the murder of George Peters and trial of Gerhard Wolf started with a full review of newspaper coverage of the crime and trial. The original court manuscripts weren't available for the research of this book, as too many years had transpired to have the records saved and accessible. Online forums on Port Burwell and Vienna history led to the discovery of George Peters's friends, who were able to provide details about George's life and other friends.

George and Anna had many relatives who were in Mexico at the time of the trial or attended but couldn't understand the trial, as they didn't speak English. Individual conversations with Tootsie, Gerhard Wolf and some of his children, and other family members were how I compiled the stories of their lives to form the basis of this book. The research and family and friends who shared memories of George and Anna were added after each newspaper article.

The police stayed with George's body until after the autopsy, as no bullet was found in the car. It was later found embedded in his liver, which caused him to slowly bleed to death.

George Peters is the "John Peters" in this article.

News spread around Port Burwell the morning George's body was found.

CHAPTER TWENTY: ANALYSIS OF NEWSPAPER ARTICLES AND TRIAL

A former coworker of George's recalled: "I got the phone call telling me what had happened to George, and the Vienna Hotel owners were totally devastated by the news when I called them. Knowing George like we did, it was very hard to believe that something like that could happen to a person like him. You can rest assured that there were many people who were totally devastated and saddened by the news. He was liked a great deal by everyone."

The driver of the car wasn't from the area and had only met George on one or two occasions. The newspaper interviewed farm owners near where the car had gotten stuck, and they denied ever hearing anyone knock on the door. The storm that night left next to zero visibility, and with the driver not knowing the area, he was quickly disoriented and wandered in the back roads, trying to find help.

"I can tell you they weren't partying, not in that house." Gerhard and Margaret Wolf were known in the community as strict Mennonites, and based on this quote from the police officer's statement, they had made it clear to him that their religious values were very important to them.

Gerhard and Margaret Wolf and the Influence of the Old Colony Mennonite Church

In the Reinland Fellowship Mennonite Church on Glencoln Line in Aylmer, George Peters was given a Mennonite funeral. Gerhard Wolf was released from jail to attend the funeral of the man he had murdered. The elders of the church were witnessed by another inmate to have been to jail to see Gerhard and were instrumental in finding legal counsel for him. During my research, I found someone who attended Gerhard's first bail hearing.

"When Gerhard made his first court appearance after the shooting, I was in court. Gerhard's court appearance was the first one on the docket that morning. He was led into the courtroom handcuffed in the custody of two OPP officers. There was a legal aid lawyer there to speak for Gerhard, and his first appearance took all of maybe ten to fifteen minutes. He was asked to stand up in the prisoner's box where he was seated, and the judge read off the murder charges to Gerhard and asked him if he wished to make a plea of guilty or not guilty at that time. The legal aid lawyer answered for Gerhard, stating that he didn't wish to make a plea at that time, as Gerhard's chosen legal counsel (legal aid appointed) would need more time to first go over his case and the evidence against him."

"The crown attorney made a few suggestions as to dates for Gerhard's next court appearance, the judge set bail for $5,000, and Gerhard was led back out shortly afterwards. Gerhard was looking extremely solemn that morning to say the least, but he also appeared to have a scowl on his face, like he was thinking at that moment that he shouldn't even have been charged or brought into court for what he had done. When Gerhard was led out of the courtroom and back to jail, three Mennonite men in dark suits walked out of the courtroom. These were the same men that often came into the hotel to pay the tabs of Mennonites who had money owing. The community secretly called them the 'enforcers,' as these men made sure their congregation followed the rules and didn't damage the reputation of the colony in the community."

They would be a big part of the trial, acting as his interpreter while also writing Margaret's and Anna's statements. When Gerhard was allowed out of jail to attend his brother-in-law's funeral, it was a strong, strategic move on the part of the church and his lawyer to demonstrate that he was a good Christian man who still had faith in God and was still accepted as part of his congregation. This would set up the public perception that the Old Colony church was part of George's and Gerhard's lives and ensure that the public didn't question the decision of one of their own members, Gerhard, to shoot George instead of seeking guidance through prayer and congregation support in a religious group known as pacifists.

The hierarchy of the Mennonite church was that the elders or a deacon would hire, coach, and direct the pastor and any devoted congregation members to lead a life that was above reproach. The persons in these elected roles would then be appointed to preach and teach with authority, using words from the scriptures to ensure faithful living and devotion to God.

The ministerial team was responsible for interpreting the Bible and setting the standards within each colony and how they should live everyday, which included when to access healthcare or counselling resources. Each minister had control over how to interpret the Bible in relation to the health concerns that his congregation was experiencing, and then how those people would be treated by others. It would help explain why George and Anna hadn't been

CHAPTER TWENTY: ANALYSIS OF NEWSPAPER ARTICLES AND TRIAL

attending church when they came to Ontario despite Old Colony churches being in their area.

Anna was one of eight children, and Gerhard was nine years older than her. When Anna was fifteen years old, their father died from liver failure related to alcoholism. Gerhard had a lot of responsibly to ensure that Anna met the rules of her congregation and family, and although he was ashamed of her behaviour, he was still bound to be her protector as one of the men of the family. Shooting George would have been an act of defending his sister's honour.

Many years after the shooting, when I was speaking to his children and sharing my side of the experience, they would often say they didn't know anything about the life we led. Gerhard hadn't understood that George was working long hours while Anna, due to her mental illness, was feeding her addiction with alcohol and prostitution.

I had been put up for adoption at the age of nine years old, so my relationship with my birth family was nonexistent. However, I was able to meet and speak with my Uncle Gerhard. I had just begun searching for my siblings and family when I had found his name in the telephone book.

I was at his home, and his children greeted me. He refused to speak to me in English. He spoke in Plautdietsch with his children translating. He cried during the whole visit. The family wanted to know what became of George's children. I didn't know any Plautdietsch and spoke in English, which everyone seemed to accept. Gerhard appeared heartbroken so many years after the murder. I needed to see him, forgive his decisions in that moment, and understand what kind of a man he was. His refusal to speak directly to me or meet my eyes made a lasting impression on me of his life of guilt and shame. He eventually left the room, leaving me with his wife, Margaret.

There would be very little chance of Margaret Wolf having $5,000 to put forward as bail, so I suspect the Old Colony Mennonite Church paid these fees to get him released. This article was from May 1972, five months after he was put in jail. This would mean that outside of their government cheques, Margaret and Anna were now living with no financial income except for that which Margaret's children could earn working in the nursery or fields. They don't discuss Gerhard having an interpreter present for the bail hearing, but based on the trial information, it seems that there was a church elder present who translated proceedings from English to Plautdietsch.

This article calls George Peters "John" in error. The trial would begin in September of 1972.

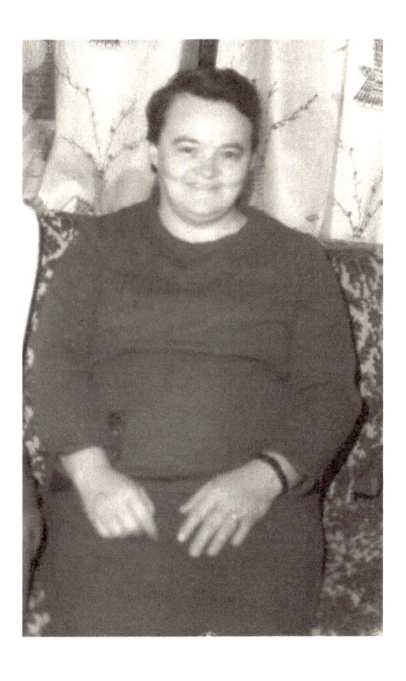

Anna after her stay in the St. Thomas Psychiatric hospital.

Anna Peters "felt in her heart" that her brother would shoot her husband when he came to the house on January 2nd. This indicated that she knew of the gun and Gerhard's intent. She claims that her brother was the only one upstairs at the time of the shooting, which is clearly inaccurate, as Anna and twelve children were upstairs together in one room. If Anna had seen a gun "locked" upstairs in one of the rooms, it would be very unlikely she would have understood that it was locked. Despite being a pacifist, Mennonite woman who never had seen or touched a weapon in her life, she is still quoted in this newspaper article as being involved in the discussion of the gun, knowing about it, and also viewing George on the night that he entered the Wolf home. When the fighting started on the main floor, Anna could hear her husband's voice and hid inside the closet in case he tried to find her.

When the gun was fired, she stayed in the closet but screamed. After the kids were mostly away and running to the bedroom door to look outside the window, Anna emerged from the closet but didn't go downstairs right away.

CHAPTER TWENTY: ANALYSIS OF NEWSPAPER ARTICLES AND TRIAL

When the children saw the driver and George get in the car and drive away, she went to look down the stairs to see what was happening and screamed again. She was crying and yelling when she saw the blood, and Gerhard and Margaret silenced her as Gerhard called the police to tell them that he had shot George.

One important fact to consider in Anna's testimony is that at the time it was given, it had been nine months since the murder. She had been living with the Wolfs during this time and was receiving coaching on the events of the night. She would have been in shock, her voices would have been unmanageable in trying to help her come to terms with this stress in her life, and she would have been seeking alcohol to help calm her nerves. After years of drinking pure alcohol, she would have had withdrawal symptoms, brain and organ damage, and poor memory.

Many years later, during conversation with Anna when she was homeless on the streets of Windsor, she talked about the trauma of having her husband killed by her brother. She would ruminate on why he would have done that to her husband and talk about how this was her fault because she "told some stories to Gerhard to get myself out of trouble, then I lost my kids." Until the day of her death, she would randomly tear up when thinking of George and say, "Why did he have to die like that? He never loved me, but he was a good man."

Anna had significant mental health symptoms and addiction on the night of the shooting and for years after. Her testimony would have had to have been coached to be as clear as the newspaper states. She also didn't speak very much English and not very clearly, but the newspaper doesn't indicate that she required an interpreter for her testimony. Until her death, her English was very broken, and she would often mix in Plautdietsch words to make up for those she didn't know in English.

When Anna was asked about whether she received beatings from George, it was based on the defense she originally gave her brother to cover up her actions. She had come up with a story to support her leaving her home with her children in the winter night and to explain her bruises from a recent assault by a man she had brought into her home for sex. George wasn't visiting Anna very often and wasn't witnessed by any of her children to have hit her hard enough to cause bruises in several years.

George's friends' comments:

"Any witness who testified in court during that trial after holding the Bible and taking the oath to tell the truth that George Peters was a violent man was an outright liar and should have been cross-examined to the limit by the crown attorney to bring out the 'true character' in them."

"In any dictionary, beside the words 'gentle giant,' there should be a photo of George Peters, because that's exactly what he was: a big, gentle, and kind-hearted giant."

The Driver of the Car

"Marshy," Mr. Marshall, had no relationship with George. He was a general labourer and had recently found the Vienna Hotel to have a beer after work. He was a hardworking young man whose father operated a business outside of the area. He was working as a labourer in the tobacco barns for extra money while his family business wasn't as busy. Mr. Marshall was being kind and helpful to George that night when he drove him to Gerhard's home. He had a lot to drink at the bar and also offered beer to George, which I believe he took. In the end, Mr. Marshall ended up in a situation no one would want to be in—lost in a snowstorm with a gunshot victim. He did the best that he could in getting help, but he wasn't able to find it in time to save George's life.

Friend's statement:

"If George was conscious, he would have been giving Mr. Marshall directions, and given the fact that Mr. Marshall was trying to save George's life, he would have been asking directions from George. After leaving the vehicle, Mr. Marshall would have had close to five miles to walk to get to the farmhouse. Unfortunately, he took what he thought was a shortcut through a heavily wooded area on an old logging road, and when the logging road came to a dead end in the middle of the woods, he was totally lost and tramped around in the woods the better part of that night."

Gerhard and Margaret Wolf had called the police that evening multiple times, stating that they would shoot George if the police didn't stop him from coming to their home. This information is from a very reliable source and is not part of the court reporting. Gerhard had a loaded gun ready for George's arrival that he had taken from an upstairs closet before his arrival; he shot George

CHAPTER TWENTY: ANALYSIS OF NEWSPAPER ARTICLES AND TRIAL

from the bottom of the stairs. His children witnessed these acts. "When I aim for something, I usually hit it."

He did hit his target that night and felt justified and confident in his right to do this, as he called the police himself to state, "No need to come and stop George. I just stopped him. He is shot." Neither the officers nor his wife noted any remorse. George hadn't pushed his way into the home or toppled Margaret Wolf. She may have fallen, but it was because George was insistent on getting his children that night and was a big man who made it clear what his intent was.

The officer stated that there were no grounds for complaints on the many occasions that he was called to the Peters household. No one had investigated enough to find out that many times, it was due to strangers assaulting Anna in her home after sexual acts, children going to call the police, or CAS being called to take their children for neglect.

In the perceived abuse and chaos of this night, Margaret, a frail, Plautdietsch-speaking woman, was able to write down the license plate number of the driver's car and report it to police. It took her some time to find a pen, memorize a number, and write it down when there was blood running down the stairs of her home and her husband was holding a smoking gun. There was premeditation from the Wolf couple. Previously, they had called for the OPP to search for George's car, as he had called to let them know he would be coming over. It's hard to understand how this traumatic event would allow enough calmness to be able to determine it wasn't George's car and that a license plate would be needed to find George after the shooting.

The other important fact is: Why would a Mennonite man, living on the grounds of a greenhouse, have a gun and feel confident in loading and using it?

Court read admission accused shot his brother-in-law

An admission, signed by Gerhard Wolfe, 39, of RR 1, Port Burwell, that he shot his brother-in-law, George Peters, 32, of Vienna, Ontario, early in the morning of January 2, this year, was read Friday to an Ontario Supreme Court jury.

But in the admission, Wolfe said that he thought his shot struck Peters in the left arm, although he added that Peters might have moved just as he fired.

Peters was, in fact, wounded in the left chest, and died from loss of blood when the car taking him to hospital became stuck in a ditch and wasn't found until six hours later.

Wolfe, charged with non-capital murder in connection with the shooting, took the stand, himself, Friday, to say that both he and his sister, Anna, the victim's wife, were frightened of Peters.

Speaking through an interpreter, Wolfe said that he had seen Peters fight as many as five men at one time when they lived in their native Mexico.

He said that his sister told him Peters had beaten her and their six children and said that he had seen bruises on their bodies.

Elgin County Crown Attorney Douglas Walker completed his case after two days, Friday, with the submission of the written statement.

Defence testimony was adjourned to resume Monday. It is expected that the case will go to the jury of eight women and four men sometime later in the day.

In a verbal statement to police, shortly after the shooting, Wolfe reportedly said that he had twice threatened to shoot Peters if he didn't leave the house, and Peters refused both times.

When he made one of the two threats, Wolfe was reportedly holding a rifle.

But in the written statement, dictated and signed by Wolfe, and in testimony given by his sister, Anna, no such warning was mentioned.

Mrs. Peters told the court that her brother didn't say anything to her husband before going upstairs where the rifle was kept, moments before a shot rang out at the top of the stairs and her husband grabbed at his chest.

The court was told earlier that Peters, in a drunken state, appeared at the Wolfe house about 3 a.m. demanding to see his estranged wife, who was hiding in one of the bedrooms. Wolfe said that Peters had been living with another woman in Tilsonburg at the time, having separated from Anna Peters three months earlier.

In the written statement, Wolfe said that his wife let Peters into their home after he kept kicking at the door. He said that Peters kept shoving his wife backwards until she was near the telephone.

She tried to call the police, the statement continued,, but Peters put his hand on the hook and said "you'd better not".

Wolfe said he then went upstairs, got the rifle, loaded it, and came back to the head of the stairs and saw Peters still standing near the telephone at the foot of the stairs.

Wolfe said he then pointed the rifle and "I guess he started to walk. I was scared but I pulled the trigger. If I'm right I shoot him in the left arm." Then he walked out slowly."

Wolfe said that Peters stopped in the rear doorway, and was told he'd have to leave. He fell down the step and got into a car which then left.

While testifying, Wolfe said that he didn't have too much to do with Peters since the families came to Canada in 1966, because "I was afraid of him and he was a man to fear."

"I did not want to argue with him. I had seen too much of what he had done. He had fought as many as five men. He was not afraid of anyone."

Wolfe has been provided with an interpreter since the trial opened, Wednesday, because his lawyer, William Johnson of St. Thomas said that his command of the English language was somewhat limited.

"Mr. Wolfe hasn't sufficient command of the English language to instruct me and I have always used a translator in dealing with him.

But police officers have testified that while Wolfe's grammar is frequently not correct they generally had little difficulty in understanding him or making themselves understood.

His statement was written down by police and read back to him before he signed it because he could neither read nor write in English, police said.

Members of the jury asked Friday, if it were possible to hear Wolfe's testimony directly without an interpreter in light of what the police had said.

But the presiding judge, Madame Justice Mabel Margaret Van Camp of the Ontario Supreme Court pointed out that the defence was allowed to conduct its case in the manner it felt was most fair to the accused.

"It is most important," she said, "that the accused understand exactly what he is being asked and that you hear, as accurately as possible, what his answers are."

A Mexican-born Mennonite, Wolfe speaks and understands a dialect known as Low German best. Mr. Johnson said. Wolfe has said that although he speaks German at home, he has spoken in English while working at McConnell's Nursery in Port Burwell for the past five years.

The jury questioned Gerhard Wolf's need for an interpreter. He was a full-time employee and supervisor of a nursery, managing workers and scheduling. He could speak fluent English but, as probably advised by his Old Colony church elders, he had insisted that he couldn't speak the language. In court documents, it's noted that he hadn't had a relationship with George and his family since 1968. He stated that based on his sister's account, she was abused, and he saw bruises on the occasion that she ended up at his home. He presumed them to be from George, but this was inaccurate.

The lawyers didn't ask more about his relationship with George throughout their lives, but Gerhard and George were described by relatives as "best friends." What would then lead to Gerhard using a gun to threaten George when he arrived at his home? One explanation would be that Gerhard had a strong relationship with the church, and he feared excommunication if his family didn't meet their moral standards.

When Gerhard died, he was buried in the same cemetery as his best friend, George. It was not a Mennonite cemetery.

CHAPTER TWENTY: ANALYSIS OF NEWSPAPER ARTICLES AND TRIAL

George's Girlfriend

Mennonite couples rarely divorced. It was frowned upon by their religion, and even if they found new partners, they would maintain their marriages, often until death. George finding a woman to love and who loved and respected him in turn would have been a wonderful part of his life, but he also had a wife who suffered from severe mental illness and addictions who he was helpless to seek treatment for.

From what I've read and researched, George's girlfriend didn't testify at his trial. I was able to speak to her on the phone many years after the shooting, and she talked about how kind he was and how he really wanted only the best for his children. A few days before he was killed, while working at the hotel, he'd heard that Anna was having sex with local farmers and also offering her daughters for the same. George had been saving money to get a better home for his children, and he made a choice on January 2, 1972, at 3 a.m. that he could no longer leave his children in the care of his wife.

Tootsie attended George's funeral. She was remembered as someone who "worshipped the ground that George walked on."

In the testimony summary, a lot of attention is paid again to the language barrier that Gerhard faced, but there is no mention that Old Colony Mennonite Church members acted as his interpreter and that their words may not have been Gerhard's. They had already committed $5,000 to his release and were fighting to maintain their reputation during this trial. The information about Anna's beatings and Gerhard witnessing bruises was never questioned, despite the fact that Gerhard hadn't seen Anna and George for over three years. There were no witnesses to her abuse or how she was harmed.

Gerhard's lawyer turned the murder trial around to focus on Anna's testimony and her abuse. It took the motive and premeditation of harm out of the story by drawing sympathy to the battered, simple Mennonite wife. The jury included eight women—which was strategic, as Anna's testimony was the focus of this murder trial. The defense wouldn't question her mental state and words.

No witnesses were called to defend George's character. Gerhard Wolf "accidently fired" a loaded gun when there was conversation within the home with Anna and Margaret about the gun, and Anna feared that her brother would kill her husband.

As a child of George Peters, I can say that I was never physically abused by him. He did have a temper, but I saw it only on a few occasions during conversations with my mother, and the only thing he would hit with a fist in frustration was a table or wall. I have no memory of him hitting Anna at any time. There was also no evidence brought forward at his trial of any violence while breaking up fights as part of his role as a bartender.

Friends/work colleagues:

"George was rarely drunk. He was able to manage other drunks and work as part of team to earn a good wage with dignity."

"George worked unbelievable hours to feed his family. He would put in eight hours a day at his daytime job in the greenhouses or tobacco barns. Then, he would come to work in the hotel at 6 p.m. and would put in another eight hours through to closing time at night. He did this for six days a week," according to those who worked alongside him. "He was always on time for his jobs. When he got hired full-time at the hotel, he couldn't have been happier. He could now just work one job and make as much money as doing both. He was very appreciative of the opportunity and wouldn't have done anything to jeopardize it."

"George loved his job at the bar. He was a real people person and got along well with everyone. He didn't take long to fit into this small farming community, and with most locals going to the bar after work, he was well-known. The Vienna Hotel was a pretty rough place to work, especially during the summer tobacco harvest months when all the transient tobacco help from Quebec would come in. They didn't respect anyone, and they loved a good fist fight. But George was a big man with a big face and acted with the other bartenders as bouncers. It wasn't unusual to have four to six men fighting, and they would have to be thrown out. George had the worst shift because he worked nights, and that was when most of the rowdies would show up. But George knew his coworkers were only around the corner if he needed any help managing the people.

"George was seen by his community as an easygoing, mild-mannered person. He didn't really like to have to manhandle anyone to get them to leave the premises. He would always do his very best to try and talk to the person(s) causing the problems. When the need arose, though, George had no problems whatsoever in clearing out any number of unruly patrons at one time. George always tried to negotiate before he had to physically remove people from the bar."

CHAPTER TWENTY: ANALYSIS OF NEWSPAPER ARTICLES AND TRIAL

> **ST. THOMAS, ONTARIO, TUESDAY, SEPTEMBER 12, 1972**
>
> ## Jury deliberates on non-capital murder charge
> # Four days of testimony ended
>
> Although he has been working towards a conviction for non-capital murder for four days, Elgin County Crown Attorney Douglas Walker said, Monday, that "manslaughter is the verdict most likely open to the jury" in the trial of Gerhard Wolfe, 39, of RR 1, Port Burwell.
>
> Wolfe is charged in connection with the shooting death in January of this year of his brother-in-law, George Peters, 32, of Vienna, Ontario.
>
> In his summation to the jury of eight women and four men who were to decide Wolfe's fate this afternoon, Mr. Walker described the victim of the shooting as "a reprobate, no doubt; a black sheep in the family; a menace to everybody he came into contact with."
>
> Wolfe took the stand himself, again Monday, to testify that the rifle he was holding at the time of the shooting went off accidently.
>
> Speaking through an interpreter, Wolfe said that he was coming down the stairs in his farm home with his finger on the trigger when the weapon discharged.
>
> Peters was standing at the foot of the stairs at the time and was struck in the left chest by the 22-calibre bullet. He died later from loss of blood when the car taking him to hospital became stuck in a ditch and wasn't found for six hours.
>
> Mr. Walker has rejected the argument of accidental discharge of the weapon and said that the evidence in the case is clear that Wolfe "probably intended to shoot Peters; although he didn't intend to kill him."
>
> Evidence in the trial has shown that Peters pushed his way into the Wolfe farm home about 3 a.m. on January 2 while in a drunken state. He demanded to see his estranged wife, Anna, Wolfe's sister, who was staying there at the time.
>
> Defence counsel William Johnson of St. Thomas argued in his summation to the jury that Wolfe's limited command of the English language caused him to say things to police about the shootings which were misinterpreted... including statements that he aimed the rifle at Peters before deliberately pulling the trigger.
>
> **LANGUAGE A PROBLEM**
>
> McConnell Millard, superintendent of production at the McConnell Nursery Co. Ltd. in Port Burwell where Wolfe has worked for the past five and one half years, testified, Monday, that Wolfe's grammar was poor to the point that he would "use the wrong nouns and pronouns; and put words in the wrong order which would very much tend to change the meaning of whole sentences."
>
> Wolfe, a Mexican-born Mennonite whose native tongue is a dialect known as low German, has been provided with an interpreter throughout the trial.
>
> Mr. Millard also said that when speaking to Wolfe, he found that the accused "sometimes doesn't grasp what I'm talking about", especially when the discussion involved technical language about the propagation of plants.
>
> Police officers investigating the shooting told the court earlier that, while they found Wolfe's English to be "broken", they had little difficulty in understanding him and he appeared to understand what they were asking him.
>
> Earlier in the trial, Monday, Peters was painted as a brutal, heavy-drinking man, feared by all who knew him, including Wolfe.
>
> Wolfe's wife, Margaret, who is seriously ill now and was ill in January said that even though Peters knew she was ill, he grabbed her by the left arm and had a raised beer bottle in his right hand when the shooting occurred.
>
> "I didn't know what he was going to do," she said.
>
> John Fehr, 29, a Langton-area tobacco worker who knew both the Peters and Wolfe families, testified Monday that Peters pulled him from his car last October in the driveway of the Peters' home and beat him without reason in the presence of his (Fehr's) four children.
>
> He lost two front teeth and suffered a head cut in the incident, he said.
>
> John Wolfe, 51, a brother of the accused, witnessed the beating, and both men said that Peters had been drinking at the time.
>
> John Wolfe broke into tears upon leaving the courtroom following his testimony. He spoke no English and testified through an interpreter.
>
> **SUFFERED BEATINGS**
>
> Mrs. Anna Peters, widow of the victim, testified earlier in the trial that her husband had beaten her on occasion and threatened to kill her. The court was also told that Peters' six children had suffered beatings administered by their father.
>
> Mr. Johnson took about 45 minutes in summing up his case for the jury and Mr. Walker about 18 minutes.
>
> Madame Justice Mabel Margaret Van Camp of the Ontario Supreme Court, who is presiding over the trial, offered the jury the choice of deliberating Monday evening or Tuesday afternoon. She said her charge to the jury would take an hour to 90 minutes.
>
> After a brief discussion among themselves, the jurors elected to sleep on it and come back this morning.
>
> In his summation, Mr. Walker said that "accidental shooting doesn't fit in with the evidence and there's no reasonable argument for self-defence.
>
> "He went upstairs because he was fed up with Peters and wanted to make sure he didn't come back. He had that gun loaded and ready to fire even before he saw Peters.
>
> "I'm sure he was mad and I'm not suggesting that's an unnatural reaction when a drunk comes to your door at three in the morning.
>
> "But dopes that justify shooting the man and killing him?
>
> "Was there as much violence going on there that night as you (members fo the jury) have been asked to believe?"
>
> Mr. Johnson said that "there is absolutely no evidence of murder; and a finding of manslaughter is not justified because Wolfe didn't use any more force than was necessary to remove Peters from his house."

George was described to the jury as a "black sheep," "reprobate," and "a menace to anyone he came in contact with." Gerhard Wolf found the words to say the gun went off accidently and even described a scene that didn't occur, in which he was upstairs. There's no mention of the room full of children who were in the home and witnessed the murder. The defense stated that Wolf's testimony to the police was not to be considered accurate due to his limited command of the English language, despite many people stating he could speak clearly and confidently in English. This defense, in combination with defending an abused spouse, led the jury to let Gerhard Wolf live freely. The accounts of violence from Mexico by Gerhard's brother Johan and their cousin would stand as the only proof that George could be violent.

Accused man attends funeral

Gerhard Wolf, 39, of Copenhagen was released from jail under police guard Thursday, to attend the funeral of the brother-in-law he is charged with murdering.

George Peters, 32, of Vienna, Ont., died of a single bullet wound in the chest early on the morning of January 2. He apparently came to the home of his brother-in-law, located on Elgin County Road 19.

Peter's estranged wife and six children lived in the Wolf home.

Wolf is charged with non-capital murder in the slaying and is due to appear in Provincial Judge's Court in St. Thomas, anuary 10, for plea.

Two OPP officers from the St. Thomas detachment accompanied the accused to the funeral service for Peters Thursday afternoon. The funeral was at Glencoln, located between Aylmer and Springfield, on Concession 8 of Malahide Township.

Brother-in-law charged in slaying of Elgin man

By ISAAC TURNER
of The Free Press

PORT BURWELL — A Malahide Township man died of a gunshot wound Sunday morning after being shot in a house where his estranged wife and six children were living.

John Peters, 32, believed to be of Vienna, died soon after he was shot in the chest with a .22-calibre bullet in the home of his brother-in-law, Gerhard Wolfe.

Wolfe, 39, brother of the dead man's wife, is an employee of McConnell Nursery Co. Ltd. and lives in one of the firm's houses on Elgin County Road 42 near Copenhagen.

He has been arrested and charged with non-capital murder and is scheduled to appear in St. Thomas provincial judge's court this afternoon.

According to Chief Inspector D. D. Higley of the OPP criminal investigation branch, Toronto, Peters called at Wolfe's home shortly before 3 a.m., when the shooting took place.

At the time, the house was occupied by Peters' family as well as Wolfe's wife and children.

Soon after being shot, Peters was taken from the house by an unidentified man, placed in a car and driven about 12 miles from the scene before the vehicle went off the road and into a ditch.

Inspector Higley said the man was a close friend of Peters' who had accompanied him to the house. However, he would not identify him, saying the man will be an important witness.

He said the two men were apparently headed for hospital. When the car went off the road, the unidentified man went to seek help at a neighboring house and when he returned Peters was dead.

The body and car were found a few yards from the tobacco farm home of John Engelhardt Jr., about 3½ miles west of Vienna.

Mrs. Engelhardt told The Free Press neither she nor her husband was disturbed during the night by anyone seeking assistance.

"We didn't hear anything," she said. "If anybody had tried to get us, the dog would have wakened us."

Inspector Higley described the Wolfes and Peters as Mennonites who had come to Canada from Mexico about six years ago. Large numbers of Mennonites moved from Manitoba to Mexico during the 1920s.

Questioned about the circumstances surrounding the incident, the inspector said, "I can tell you they weren't partying ... not in that house."

The inspector said Wolfe accompanied him and St. Thomas OPP Constable B. A. Thompson to St. Thomas where the arrest was made. A .22-calibre rifle owned by Wolfe has been seized.

A post mortem examination performed at Tillsonburg General Hospital showed Peters died of a single wound in the upper-left side of his chest.

Mrs. Peters learned of her husband's death when the arrest was made about 3 p.m.

CHAPTER TWENTY: ANALYSIS OF NEWSPAPER ARTICLES AND TRIAL

Man remanded in death

Free Press St. Thomas Bureau

ST. THOMAS — Gerhard Wolf, 39, of RR 1, Port Burwell, charged with non-capital murder in the Jan. 2 shooting death of his brother-in-law in a farm home near Copenhagen, was remanded in custody to Jan. 10 when he appeared in provincial court Monday.

Wolf, who entered no plea, was represented by St. Thomas lawyer William W. Johnson.

The charge was laid by St. Thomas provincial police after George Peters, 32, believed to be of Vienna, died soon after he was shot in the chest with a .22-calibre bullet in Wolf's home.

Wolf, brother of the dead man's wife, occupied the farm home with his wife and family. Also in the home were Peters' estranged wife and six children.

An autopsy performed at Tillsonburg District Memorial Hospital showed Peters died from a single wound in the upper left side of his chest.

Investigation is continuing into the incident.

Following is the time line for the night of the shooting based on first-hand accounts:

- It's already a known fact that George was working the bar at the Vienna Hotel that evening, along with the owner of the hotel and three waiters.

- At about 1:30 or 2 a.m., George called the Wolf home to let them know that he was coming to pick up his children.

- The OPP from Port Burwell went to meet with Gerhard at the house. Gerhard was really upset and angry, and it took a while to get him settled down enough to get the whole story out of him as to what was actually going on. The police officer assured Gerhard that he would do everything that he could to find George and warn him that he would be charged with trespassing if he went to the residence that night. Gerhard stated clearly then and there that if George came back, he was going to shoot him.

- There was dialogue between police forces over whose territory the Wolf home was in, and officers were reassigned. When they were on their way to his home, they received a call from Mr. Wolf at about 3 a.m. stating that he had already shot George.

- George was a big man, and in many cases, men George's size can drink a lot of alcohol before they get totally inebriated. It's a fact that George worked the Vienna Hotel bar the night of his murder. One stipulation of bartending for the Vienna Hotel bar was that anyone running the bar itself wasn't allowed to drink alcohol during the hours they were behind the bar because if the government LCBO hotel inspector happened to drop in for one of their unexpected, unannounced visits and determine that the bartender was drunk on duty, that inspector could shut the bar down immediately, fine the hotel, and even pull the hotel license for a number of days if it was an ongoing occurrence.

- ▸ If George was as drunk and miserable as Gerhard stated to the police, that means George would have had to guzzle back a large amount of alcohol in a very short time. George worked until closing time, which was 1 a.m., the time allotted by law to have everyone cleared out of the bar and all alcohol off the tables. Then, there was always an extra half hour of work to get the bar and beverage rooms ready for the cleaning crew to come in later and then for the bartender taking over the noon to 6 p.m. shift the following day.
- ▸ It was around 2 a.m. when the first call from Gerhard came, stating that George was drunk and heading over to his home and that he feared for his life. That would have given George around a half hour to get totally drunk. This wasn't true.

- People that knew George after a few drinks said they had seen George sitting at a table among friends many times and drink for two hours or more, and yet even when he was ready to leave, his mood had never changed. You would never know that the man had had a drink as far as his speech, mobility, or anything else about his movements or demeanour would suggest.

- Gerhard also told the police that George kicked the door in to enter the house, another statement that could have been easily challenged by the crown attorney. Anyone could have kicked the door in after the event to make it appear that George had actually done it. Mr. Marshall had walked in with George for a friendly visit. There would have been no need to kick the door in.

CHAPTER TWENTY: ANALYSIS OF NEWSPAPER ARTICLES AND TRIAL

- Mr. Marshall testified that George had said, "I didn't come to start any trouble. I just brought a bottle with me to have a New Year's drink with yous, and then we're leaving." Mr. Marshall would have had to follow George into the house to hear what he said to Gerhard. People who knew George's character stated he wouldn't have left Mr. Marshall sitting outside in the car while he went inside and had drinks with his wife and Gerhard. He would have invited him to go along with him, especially since it was a very cold and stormy winter night.

- The only people downstairs to open the door for George were Gerhard and Margaret. Their children, Anna, and her children were all upstairs in the bedroom. The gun was retrieved from the upstairs room prior to George's arrival, and if it was originally locked, it had been removed; the gun was loaded and ready for his arrival.

- The children heard noises in the home. The bedroom door was open, and George was calling for his children to come to him. Gerhard shot him in front of his children and his own family. He then kicked him outside the front door as he tried to leave. He calmly called the OPP to state that they'd be able to "find my brother-in-law now because I've just shot him." George had taken off in the car, but Gerhard still had the gun.

ACKNOWLEDGEMENTS

I was present for my father's murder, and I relived that evening for many years on the anniversary of his death. I thought of what I could have done better and what more could have been done to make sure his voice was heard at his trial. After his death, I was whisked away; shortly after the trial ended, I was placed up for adoption. I insisted that I be placed with my two younger brothers, as I had been caring for them since their birth. I wouldn't see my other siblings again for many years. My siblings were in this with me, but this research and writing was from my heart. The years apart during our childhoods and after our father's death would create a distance we could never reconnect completely. Still, we celebrated many holidays together over the years, even though our lives were very different.

I tucked the memories of my past away, and I was encouraged to not speak of them and instead focus on my new family and life. That was easier said than done as I matured, with the triggers in my life that gave me glimpses into a past I tried to discredit or pretend were fabricated to avoid the truth they revealed.

My adoptive parents, Keith and Helena Dawson, provided a safe home with consistency, patience, and support. They longed for children, as they were unable to have their own, and they saw our ready-made family as a blessing to the farm home. They were able to raise George and Anna's youngest three children to adulthood. They took on the massive task of bringing us three into their home and raising us without fully knowing about the trauma and developmental challenges we would face. Until their final breaths, they remained committed

ACKNOWLEDGEMENTS

to their duties as our parents. They were brave, courageous, and supportive throughout our lives. Without their love, this story would not be written.

My parents knew about my birth parents, and we sometimes talked about them. They were aware of my meeting with my birth mother, her death, and how it impacted me and my siblings. When my adoptive mother Helena was on her deathbed, she whispered, "Write your book." She knew it was important to me, and she gave me her blessing. And so, it is done.

In my life of insecurity and moving, I was blessed to meet a good friend in public school. I had come from a life of inconsistent schooling, and it was a big transition to an English-speaking room of children who already had relationships in their young lives. Yet I met a young boy in Grade 3 who was kind, expected nothing of me, treated me fairly, and showed me how to be Canadian. This boy would be my friend throughout public school and high school. He would allow me to trust him enough to share my story in bits and pieces. It would take years for me to learn that he was supportive and loved me. My life of multiple foster homes and an unstable childhood home meant he had to try harder to earn my trust, but he stood by me, even when I pushed him away. He heard my stories and then went through microfilm to find the articles of my father's murder and trial. It was with him that I read them for the first time when I was in high school. I slowly processed the information, reread it, and began to understand that my glimpses into my past were real.

This man, Tom, would eventually become my husband. His love would give me the strength to open each newspaper article, remember my life, and start writing about the events. Our children would be vital to that process, as I could see my father's characteristics in each of them, and I knew that their lives would be enriched with the knowledge of their history. I am now blessed to have daughters-in-law, grandchildren, and an enriched life because of the love and support Tom gave me from my teens to adulthood to tell my story honestly and without shame. His natural curiosity pushed me to find relatives, make contacts who knew my father, and put my shame aside and focus on telling my father's story the way he would have wanted it.

My father, George, would never know that his friend Wayne would be by his side for his work in the bar and his murder trial. He would never know that Wayne then got to know his daughter and share his memories of their lives together with her. Wayne was a devoted friend through his life and death. He helped me to know my father, his loves, his passions, and his faults. I will be forever grateful for this opportunity. He would tear up looking at photos of my sons and how much they reminded him of my father. This connection to the father I remembered would empower me to continue writing and researching. His words of encouragement would help me see the good that was in this man and bring those stories and memories forward. His connections to other friends of my father's and witnesses to his life and death would allow me to fully understand his life, hopes, and dreams.

My cousin Nancy Friedrichson helped me understand my family, culture, trauma, and how our parents suffered so much in keeping their Mennonite faith. Our mothers were sisters. As her own life was just as challenging as my own, we were able to openly share our stories, and we got to know each other. She's my family, and I'm proud to be part of hers.

I met many relatives who helped me understand what my parents and grandparents took pride in, covered up, and learned to live with. These secrets are not just in my family or just in Mennonite families. Opening the scars to see the impurities will ensure that the next generations understand they can make a change starting NOW.

Thank you to my independent editor Meghan Negrijn for reading my manuscript and telling me it was a story that needed to be shared. She coached me to find a way to make my tragedy a story that others may find meaning in. Her confidence led me to move my manuscript forward to copy editing and publication.

> "Between stimulus and response there is a space. In that space is our power to choose our response. In our response lies our growth and our freedom."
>
> —Victor Frankl

ABOUT THE AUTHOR

Maria Moore was born in Mexico but she has spent her life in southwestern Ontario. She has had a fulfilling career as a registered nurse with a focus on mental health, addictions and advocacy. She enjoys hiking, storytelling and writing, With her first book, she hopes to bring awareness of the specific traumas and abuse in the private world of Mennonites and make it safe to disclose and seek treatment without shame.

She currently resides in Grand Bend, Ontario with her husband where they enjoy walks on the beach with their dogs.

Printed in Canada